CONTENTS

VAMPIRES
RESTLESS CREATURES OF THE NIGHT

Jean Marigny

DISCOVERIES

HARRY N. ABRAMS, INC., PUBLISHERS

"Get out, I tell you…. [Your place is] where, by judgment given, heads are lopped and eyes gouged out, throats cut, and by the spoil of sex the glory of young boys is defeated, where mutilation lives, and stoning, and the long moan of tortured men spiked underneath the spine and stuck on pales…. The whole cast of your shape is guide to what you are, the like of whom should hole in the cave of the blood-reeking lion…."

Aeschylus
The Eumenides, 5th century BC

CHAPTER I
BLOOD LUST

People all over the world make sacrificial offerings of blood. To keep evil spirits at bay, many cultures construct frightening idols. Right: A wooden sculpture with tusks from the Nicobar Islands. Opposite: An 18th-century Indian miniature depicting human and animal sacrifices.

Fascination with Blood in the Popular Imagination

The specific attribute of the vampire that sets it apart from other supernatural creatures of the night is that, to exist, it must drink the blood of living beings. The vampire myth was unquestionably born of fantasies linked to blood, that precious fluid that symbolizes the vital force and whose loss poses a mortal threat. The origins of these fantasies can be found in the most ancient reaches of human history. One early tangible trace was discovered in Persia (now Iran)—a prehistoric vase ornamented with a drawing of a man struggling with a monstrous creature that is trying to suck his blood. Another clue, the Babylonian myth of Lilitu—a deity known for sucking the blood of babies—while less ancient, certainly dates back thousands of years. Some authorities have placed the earliest legends of "living dead," or revenant, blood drinkers in China in the 6th century BC. Without venturing to name such a precise geographic and chronological origin, one might say that humans have always peopled their imaginary universe with bloodthirsty supernatural beings. Proof can be found in the legends not only of ancient China but also of India, Malaysia, and Polynesia, as well as those common among the Aztecs and the Eskimos. The vampire proper, however, is the product of European civilization, and to discover its roots one must turn to ancient

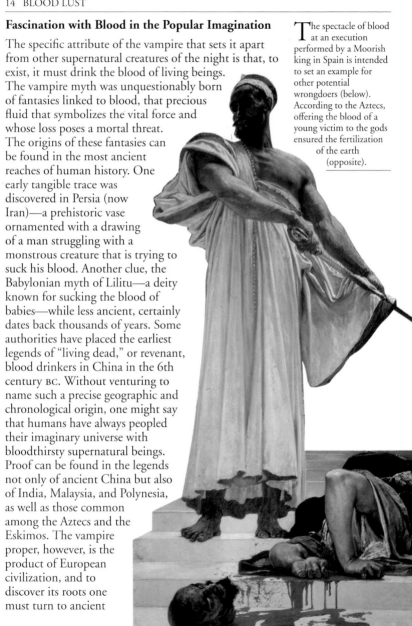

The spectacle of blood at an execution performed by a Moorish king in Spain is intended to set an example for other potential wrongdoers (below). According to the Aztecs, offering the blood of a young victim to the gods ensured the fertilization of the earth (opposite).

Greece, the cultural cradle of Western civilization, as well as to the Judeo-Christian tradition, the basis of the Western code of ethics.

Blood and Death in Greek and Latin Mythology

The ancient Greeks established a rather mysterious bond between blood and the world of the dead. In Book XI of Homer's *Odyssey*, for example, written in the 9th or 8th century BC, the wandering hero Odysseus sacrifices some sheep and collects their blood in order to call up ghosts who can help him on his journey. These spirits of the dead talk with Odysseus after drinking the sacrificial blood, which temporarily gives them back their force and vigor. To judge from other legends and cult practices, belief in blood's revitalizing ability seems to have remained strong until the Christian era.

B elow: In a scene from Greek mythology, the enchantress Medea prepares to rejuvenate her lover, Jason, by boiling him with herbs. According to Greek myth, sacrificial blood was also an elixir of youth.

Greek and Roman mythology also includes a large number of bloodthirsty goddesses, such as the empusae, lamiae, and striges. According to classical sources, Empusa, daughter of the goddess Hecate, is a demonic creature with bronze feet who can transform herself into a beautiful young woman to seduce men as they sleep. Lamia, reputed to be the daughter of an ancient oriental king named Belus, took vengeance on the murder of her children by Hera, jealous wife of Zeus, Lamia's lover, by turning into a monster that devours children or sucks their blood. (Over the centuries, the names Empusa and Lamia became the general terms *empusae* and *lamiae,* meaning witches or demons.) The striges are female demons with the bodies of birds that suck the blood of newborns in their cradles and drain sleeping men of their vitality.

These mythological creatures, like modern-day vampires, suck the blood of sleeping victims. However, there is no direct link between these ancient divinities and the vampire of today, despite the resemblance between the words *strige* and *strigoï,* the term used by Romanians since the 7th century to designate vampires. Unlike modern vampires, lamiae, empusae, and striges are not "living dead" but disembodied divinities capable of taking on human appearances in order to seduce people. In this, they anticipate the Christian-era succubi, female

L amia, represented at left in a stone relief dating from the 5th century BC, is one of the earliest prefigurations of the femme fatale and the female vampire. Disguising her repulsiveness through magic, she takes on the appearance of a bewitching beauty for her lovers and, after seducing them, sucks their blood.

Lycaon, the legendary king of Arcadia, might be considered a prototype of the werewolf, a close cousin of the vampire. In the course of a cult feast, Lycaon offered a baby disguised as a dish of food to Zeus, who, in his wrath, turned Lycaon into a wolf (left). This myth evokes the cannibalistic Arcadian practice of holding a ritual banquet during which the participants commune by eating a piece of a victim sacrificed to Zeus.

The striges, women with the bodies of birds (often confused with lamiae and empusae), are also morphologically similar to the sirens of antiquity. Here, a detail of a painting of a siren on a 5th-century BC Greek water jar (below).

demons that prey on young men as they sleep, entering into sexual relations with them to the extent that, through exhaustion, they lose their potency or even die.

The Old Testament: "The Life of All Flesh Is the Blood" (Leviticus, 17:14)

An ancient incarnation of the Babylonian Lilitu can be found in traditional Hebrew texts (although the story was removed from the Old Testament): Lilith, first wife of Adam before the creation of Eve. Reputedly impatient with the first man's sexual ineptitude, Lilith left Adam to become queen of the demons and evil spirits. Like the lamiae and striges,

she sucks the blood of infants and robs young men of their vigor and potency as they sleep. In Hebraic belief, Lilith was above all guilty of transgressing the absolute taboo of Mosaic law that forbids the drinking of blood from living things: "Therefore I said unto the children of Israel, Ye shall eat the blood of no manner of flesh; for the life of all flesh is the blood thereof: whosoever eateth it shall be cut off" (Leviticus, 17:14).

In the Old Testament story, Abraham was about to sacrifice his son Isaac to God when, at the last moment, an angel stopped him, signaling God's disapproval of human sacrifice.

Hebrews have always had a complex relationship with blood, which they consider both a symbol of life and a sign of impurity. Blood has a sacred aspect, as it brings life to the body, and only God is master of life and death. At the same time, blood is linked to the curse that has plagued humanity ever since Eve, yielding to the temptation of the devil, caused the fall of humankind —the loss of menstrual blood, which was perceived as evidence of an impure wound, a punishment inflicted by God on all the descendants of Eve. In Hebrew tradition, menstrual blood is the source of a variety of woes. A menstruating woman must not be seen in public, as her presence could trigger all sorts of calamities—the bread will refuse to rise, the wine will turn to vinegar, and the crops might be lost. And under no circumstances may she have sexual relations during this time, as she is impure. To the Hebrews, blood connotes disaster and an idea of ever-present sin.

The New Testament: Christianity Redeemed Blood

The New Testament teaches that Christ saved humankind by spilling his blood. Before undergoing the martyrdom of the cross, Christ himself implicitly emphasized the redemptive value of his blood under the symbolic guise of the wine shared with his disciples at the Last Supper. As the Gospel of John emphasizes the regenerative virtues of blood, the early church fathers had to fight a literal interpretation of this meal for fear of encouraging a return to such pagan practices as human sacrifice or ritual cannibalism.

The amulet shown below was believed to protect newborn children from the terrible Lilith, a female demon that sucked the blood of babies in their cradles.

The demon goddess Lilith, derived from an ancient Babylonian myth, is linked to Genesis by a rabbinical tradition that named her the first wife of Adam. Unlike Eve, who was created from the body of the first man, Lilith, like Adam, was drawn from the earth. Spurning Adam, she turned into an evil spirit that haunted ruins and deserts.

In this German primitive painting on wood from the beginning of the 19th century, angels sprinkle Christ's precious blood on souls in purgatory awaiting the Last Judgment.

Religious leaders were not the only ones to exert their influence on this issue. Beginning in 772, Charlemagne (742–814), king of the Germanic tribe known as the Franks, made numerous attempts to subjugate the Saxons, a neighboring Germanic tribe. In 777 he was finally successful, and in 785 he announced an edict that not only forced the pagan Saxons to be baptized but punished by death those who, confusing pagan beliefs and the mystery of the transubstantiation (that is, the actual presence of Christ's flesh and blood during Communion), took part in feasts of human flesh.

Despite all such precautions, in the medieval Christian world blood was invested with supernatural powers that were easily transferable to demonology, the source of belief in vampires. In the 11th century, the idea of the redemptive value of blood and a pernicious interpretation of the cult of the Virgin Mary led witches and doctors alike to prescribe the unsullied blood of virgin girls to counter all sorts of illnesses and slow the effects of aging.

Life after Death: The "Returned in Body"

The Neoplatonic idea of a life after death constitutes another link between Christianity and belief in vampires: The body, a simple material covering, rots away, while the soul continues to live in another world, awaiting resurrection at the Last Judgment. The souls of sinners

The Eucharist, the Christian rite that symbolizes Christ's sacrifice for humankind, gave rise to sacrilegious practices inspired by black magic, as shown in this painting by 15th-century Italian artist Paolo Uccello depicting the profanation of the host.

This 15th- or 16th-century German crucifixion scene embodies intense suffering.

can be saved provided they repent and, most importantly, that they receive last rites before they die. This excludes from the possibility of salvation all those who have not received extreme unction (a sacrament during which a priest prays for the salvation of a dying person) or who were not buried in consecrated ground, such as suicides or the excommunicated. This is the source of the belief in spirits that return (revenants) and vampires, which, according to Christian logic, are literally "souls in pain," for they belong to neither the world of the living nor that of the dead. The main difference between revenants and vampires is that the former no longer have their flesh covering and are harmless, while the latter are bodies improperly inhabited by their souls, which have returned from purgatory: the "returned in body."

One of the biblical prophecies that has generated the most imaginative sparks is that of the Last Judgment, to be accompanied by the resurrection of the dead (above left). A sinner's entry to hell is gained by way of a dizzying fall guided by a demon (above right).

Hell is often represented as a furnace where demons torture the damned, as in this 19th-century Romanian icon (opposite above).

Cadaver Sanguisugus

In the 11th century, stories of corpses found intact outside their tombs began to circulate in Europe. A French specialist in the occult named Jacques Albin Simon Collin de Plancy related in his *Dictionnaire Infernal* (Diabolical Dictionary) of 1818 a report made by the bishop of Cahors, a city in central France, in 1031. According to the bishop, an excommunicated knight in his diocese who had died and been buried was spotted far from his burial

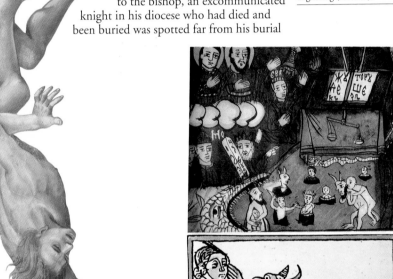

A young man who commits the transgression of opening a tomb to see once more the face of his beloved runs the risk of discovering a grimacing devil, or even a vampire. This, at least, is the lesson of this 15th-century engraving (bottom).

site more than once. The most significant examples to be found in England in the 12th century are recorded in chronicles written in Latin: *De Nugis Curialium* (Courtiers' Triflings), written between 1182 and 1192 by noted ecclesiastical scholar and wit Walter Map (c. 1140–c. 1209), and in 1196, *Historia Rerum Anglicarum* (A History of England) by William of Newburgh (1136–c. 1198), an Augustinian monk. These two works contain all manner of tales of the dead, mostly excommunicated, who leave their tombs every night to torment those close to them or to provoke a series of suspicious deaths. When their caskets are opened, their bodies are found to be intact and spotted with blood. The only way to end the evil spell, it was thought, was to burn the body after piercing it with a sword. Lacking a specific term, the English chroniclers named this type of living dead *cadaver sanguisugus,* Latin for "bloodsucking corpse." These, no doubt, are vampires, and the British Isles are thus the scene of the first manifestations of vampirism.

Epidemics and Superstitions

The phenomenon persisted into the Renaissance only sporadically, without leaving deep and lasting traces in the collective imagination. It was not until the 14th century that vampirism became truly endemic, mainly in the central European regions of eastern Prussia, Silesia, and Bohemia. The phenomenon, which up until then had only an anecdotal character, suddenly became widespread and generalized. It has been established that these spectacular manifestations of vampirism coincided with serious outbreaks of the bubonic plague in those regions. In order to avoid infection, people rushed to bury the victims of the disease, sometimes without even verifying that they were clinically dead. When the family vault was opened a few days later, the corpses might have been found to be perfectly preserved but spotted with blood. It did not take much to imagine that the corpses had become vampires, while in all probability the hapless victims suffered a long and horrible agony in their coffins

The frightful being in the 13th-century fresco above evokes the devil but also hints at the vampire.

In the Middle Ages, epidemic diseases were often considered the work of the devil. Opposite above: A French miniature entitled *Demons Spreading an Epidemic*. As can be seen in the 14th-century Italian miniature at left, the main concern of survivors was to bury the presumedly contagious dead as quickly as possible.

and wounded themselves in their vain attempts to break out of their wooden prisons. Thus, in the superstitious 14th century, the plague promoted belief in vampires in central and eastern Europe.

Two Monsters of the 15th Century

In the 14th and 15th centuries, western Europe suffered only sporadic episodes of vampirism. The 1440 trial of Gilles de Rais in France, however, was extremely well known; his name is associated with vampirism even today, thanks to 19th-century French novelist Joris-Karl Huysmans, who, in his novel *Là-bas* (1891), portrayed him as an authentic vampire.

A former member of Joan of Arc's guard and erstwhile marshal of France, Gilles de Rais (1400–40), having retired to his lands in southwest France, devoted himself to alchemy, believing he could find the secret of the

Gilles de Rais, whose seal is shown above, was the most atrocious torturer of children in history. According to Roger Villeneuve in his 1955 biography *Gilles de Rais*, Rais commanded the singing of a children's chorus to accompany the death rattles of the children he was killing.

"philosophers' stone" in blood. (The philosophers' stone was an imaginary substance believed to have the property of converting other metals into gold.) His experiments awakened brutal instincts, however, and he proceeded to kill between two and three hundred children in horrifying tortures. Although the story of Gilles de Rais corresponds more closely with the image of the ogre or of the legendary Bluebeard, he is often described as a vampire.

A historical figure even more closely associated with the vampire was Vlad Tepes (1431–76), prince of Walachia, an ancient kingdom now part of Romania. Vlad carried the double surname of Tepes (the Impaler) and Dracula (a diminutive form of Dracul, Vlad's father's name, meaning devil or dragon). Vlad was both a national hero who fought courageously to liberate his land from Ottoman invaders and a bloodthirsty tyrant who ordered thousands of people impaled solely for his pleasure.

Vlad's sinister exploits fueled numerous chronicles and made him a legendary character whose name has become inseparable from the vampire myth today. Four centuries later, his cruelty would excite the attention of Irish writer Bram (Abraham) Stoker (1847–1912) and inspire him to write a novel he called *Dracula*.

With his cold and haughty air, aquiline nose, and thick mustache, Vlad Tepes (above) looked like a younger version of Count Dracula in Bram Stoker's novel, written four centuries later. Vlad's favorite tool of torture, the stake, was used at the time by conquerors against their enemies, as shown in the engraving at left, which portrays Hungarians impaled by Turks.

The bloody punishments of Vlad Tepes were mostly reported in 15th-century chronicles written in German: "The unspeakable tortures have no equal, even among the most bloodthirsty tyrants of history, such as Herod, Nero, and Diocletian." Vlad's favorite mode of execution was impalement, the victim often having been previously torn to pieces. On these pages are two woodcuts from the 16th century.

In 1486 Pope Innocent VIII sanctioned the publication of *Malleus Maleficarum,* a treatise on the phenomena of female and male nocturnal demons—known as succubi and incubi, respectively—and revenants. The papal approval had the effect of a thunderclap. To all appearances, the Church had officially recognized the existence of the living dead. Little more was needed to unleash the spirits.

CHAPTER II
THE CONSECRATED VAMPIRE

Two 15th-century portrayals of Death triumphant: A Flemish painting (opposite) and a French woodcut (left).

The "Living Dead," Fiends from Hell

In the second half of the 16th century, the Reformation, a movement led by dissenters from Roman Catholic doctrines and practices, likewise made vampirism official. A common belief of the time, an era still beset by outbreaks of the plague, was that there were corpses that not only devoured themselves in their coffins but also had the power to cause the death of living persons at a distance, as if by magic. Some witnesses claimed to have actually heard the dead chewing in their tombs. It has been recorded that a story of this sort was related to the founder of the Reform movement, Martin Luther (1483–1546) himself, by a minister named Georg Röhrer. Starting in 1552 in Prussia and Silesia it became customary to place a stone or a coin in the mouths of the dead to prevent them from chewing. These proto-vampires were termed *Nachzehrer* in German, which may be roughly translated as "predators" or "parasites."

The two medieval illustrations below represent scenes of cruentation, that is, the ability of a corpse's wounds to bleed in the presence of its murderer. In this way the duke of Gloucester, the future Richard III and murderer of the king, was unmasked in Shakespeare's *Richard III*.

The German painter Hans Baldung Grien (c. 1484–1545) was famous for his "vanities," canvases or engravings representing beautiful young women grappling with half-decomposed cadavers. These works clearly signify the transience of youth and beauty before the inevitability of death. Less well known, however, is Grien's painting *The Knight, the Maiden, and Death* (left), in which a woman's desperate struggle against death is represented as a contest between a gallant knight and his love's deadly destiny.

In England, an act of Parliament in 1604 reinforced the repression of sorcery. In the first twelve years of James I's reign (1603 to 1615), hundreds of witches, or supposed witches, were condemned to the stake. At left is a 17th-century wood engraving of witches roasting a child.

In Switzerland, other theologians of the Reformation—including the highly influential Protestant John Calvin (1509–64)—who challenged the notion of souls in purgatory could not explain the return of the dead except by sorcery. In his 1581 tract on specters, spirits, and nocturnal spooks, Swiss theologian Louis Lavater postulated that revenants were not the souls of the dead but demons who assumed the appearance of the deceased, an idea taken up by King James VI (1566–1625) of Scotland (later king of England under the name James I), in his treatise *Demonology* (1597). The king was particularly knowledgeable in the study of the occult sciences. From this moment on, the living dead, recognized as authentic messengers of the devil, had full rights of citizenship in western European culture.

The Bloodstained Countess

Early in the 17th century, an affair strikingly similar to that of Gilles de Rais in France two centuries before strongly affected the superstitious land of Hungary: the trial of Countess Erzsebet Báthory in 1611. She was accused of having kidnapped and tortured to death numerous hapless young girls who lived in the villages surrounding her castle at Csejthe, set at the top of a hill in the mountainous region of Hungary near the Carpathians. According to contemporary chronicles, the victims numbered between eighty and three hundred; the actual count was probably closer to the latter figure. As in the cases of Gilles de Rais and Vlad Tepes, there was nothing supernatural about the

E rzsebet Báthory, in a 19th-century portrait.

affair—no one came forward to claim that the countess was one of the living dead. All the accounts agreed that she took a keen pleasure in drinking her victims' blood, which she also used to fill her bath, hoping thus to preserve her youth and looks as long as possible.

Before she embarked on her tragic career, Báthory was the neglected wife of Count Ferencz Nadasdy, a soldier renowned for his bravery. As her husband was apparently always off fighting, Báthory fought off boredom by studying black magic. With the help of Thorko, a servant who became her henchman, she began to kidnap and torture young peasant girls. After the death of her husband in 1600, Báthory devoted herself entirely to her reprehensible activities, aided by Thorko as well as her

This painting by Itsvan Csok, a 19th-century artist, shows Erzsebet Báthory viewing the torture of young girls. Her victims were beaten unremittingly, pierced with needles, bound so tightly that the ropes broke their skin, and then rolled naked in the snow.

nurse, Ilona Joo, her steward, Johannes Ujvary, and a sorceress named Darvula.

Erzsebet Báthory Became a Legend

Within a decade, dozens of young girls chained up in the castle dungeons were exquisitely tortured and bled to death. As an impressive number of young women in the area were reported missing, rumors began to spread. On 30 December 1610 Count Gyorgy Thurso, Báthory's cousin, led a detachment of soldiers and policemen to the castle just

The ruins of the castle of Csejthe, the residence of the Countess Báthory.

as one of the bloody orgies was taking place. In addition to dozens of corpses of young women, they discovered in the subterranean dungeons many live prisoners, whose bodies were covered with thousands of needle punctures, and still more prisoners who awaited their turn for such treatment.

Saved from capital punishment because of her blood ties to the royal family (her uncle was a Transylvanian prince), the countess was held captive for the remainder of her life in her own room with all the windows and doors shut. All her

The castle of Csejthe, scene of so many atrocities, was abandoned after the death of the diabolical countess. It has all the features of the quintessential gothic castle. With its thick ramparts and sinister dungeon, it most definitely served as Bram Stoker's model for Dracula's castle and is similarly situated in a dominant position in a mountainous area. Without a doubt, Countess Báthory served as the prototype for Carmilla, Count Dracula, and all the aristocratic vampires of the literature of fantasy.

accomplices, however, were executed. The castle was left deserted after the countess's death, and the spot was long believed to have been cursed.

The affair of Erzsebet Báthory gave rise to all sorts of rumors and legends in the area. In many, the countess appears to have continued after her death to indulge in bloody debaucheries, thus becoming a vampire in the true sense of the word. In any case, she is considered one of the sources for Stoker's Dracula. Erzsebet Báthory even today continues to inspire films and novels.

Vampirism Spread to the Remotest Reaches of Eastern Europe

During the 17th century, vampire-related superstitions spread southward to Albania, Bulgaria, and Greece, and eastward to the eastern part of the Austro-Hungarian Empire and Russia. Previously, almost all such incidents had originated in western Europe: Great Britain, France, Spain, and Portugal. But starting in the 16th century, these phenomena became rarer and rarer in western Europe, while they suddenly mushroomed in the east. This can be attributed to a couple of factors. The first is sociological: At the end of the 16th and the beginning of the 17th centuries, the eastern European countries were

The Tatra Mountains (pictured opposite) are the highest range in the Carpathians. These majestic mountains with almost inaccessible peaks —whose slopes might overhang deep, icy lakes or might be covered by impenetrable forests— constitute a magical and frightening terrain, fruitful ground for superstition. Bram Stoker placed Dracula's castle in a similar setting but moved it southeastward from Slovakia, in central Romania, to Transylvania.

The inhabitants of the Carpathians (below and overleaf above)—reputed to be crude, superstitious, and inhospitable— remained isolated from the modern world until very recently. Wary of strangers, they managed to keep their beliefs and traditions intact. Even today in the mountainous regions of Romania one can find houses protected from evil spirits or vampires by garlands of garlic.

The epidemic of rumors of lycanthropy preceded that of vampirism, and artists of the period were evidently not unaffected. Below is a woodcut by Lucas Cranach the Elder made in the late 15th or early 16th century. Opposite above is a 15th-century wood engraving.

poor and hard to reach, especially those in mountainous areas. The intellectual discoveries and humanist trends of the Renaissance did not travel easily to such distant lands, where, except for the middle classes living in cities, the majority of the population—consisting mainly of peasants—was illiterate. Superstitions transported orally by travelers, however, found fertile ground in these places. Another factor is religion: In countries that were predominantly Catholic—Germany, southern France,

The legend of the werewolf might have been fueled by certain hereditary disorders that caused excessive growth of hair, such as that suffered by Petrus Gonsalvus, nicknamed "the wolf-man of Bavaria," and his children. The portrait below, presented to Bohemian King Ferdinand II (1578–1637) by his nephew William V, duke of Bavaria, depicts Gonsalvus's daughter.

northern Italy, Spain, and Portugal—the Church of Rome led a pitiless struggle against heresy and superstition. Similarly, in Protestant countries such as Great Britain and Switzerland, church officials were carrying out unprecedented campaigns against witches. The Byzantine Orthodox churches in the East, on the other hand, were much more flexible in their attitudes toward superstitions, even going so far as to integrate them into their liturgy.

From *Vrykolakas* to Vampires

The Greek belief that dead people could be somehow preserved from decomposition and leave their tombs is very ancient. These "undead" were termed *vrykolakas* and comprised mostly those people who could not be buried in consecrated ground because they were suicides or for some reason had been excommunicated from the Church. Believed at first to be harmless, these troubled souls sought only to be free of their covering of flesh, and it was enough for the Church to annul its sentence of excommunication to give them peace.

Etymologically, the word *vrykolakas,* borrowed from the Slavonic language, means werewolf (that is, a human being capable of metamorphosing into a wolf), a creature that was prevalent in medieval demonology. But by the 16th century, the same word was used indiscriminately in regions of eastern Europe to refer to both the harmless living dead and the much more dangerous werewolves. The phenomenon had soon grown to such proportions throughout Europe that the Roman Catholic church decided to conduct an official investigation. Between 1520 and the mid 17th century, some thirty thousand cases of lycanthropy—human beings taking on the

English author Montague Summers (1880–1948), an authority on demonology, owned this 17th-century medallion (above, obverse and reverse) intended to keep vampires away.

forms of wolves—were reported in Europe: in the west, primarily in France; and in the east, in Serbia, Bohemia, and Hungary.

By the end of the 17th century, the rumor that after their death werewolves became living dead that sucked the blood of humans—the vampires' precursors—

became prevalent all over Silesia, Bohemia, Poland, Hungary, Moldavia, Russia, and Greece, where the once-innocuous *vrykolakas* had turned into bloodthirsty monsters. Each country had its own term to designate these formidable predators, the word *vampire* having not yet come into being. These incidents were so well known that they began to be discussed in the western European capitals, so much so that the French periodical *Le Mercure Galant,* very popular at the court of King Louis XIV, dedicated its entire October 1694 issue to the phenomenon.

At the close of the 17th century, vampirism, although it still lacked its definitive name, became a sort of collective psychosis in the countries of eastern Europe.

Peter Stubbe, a man accused of lycanthropy, was decapitated and then burned in 1589 near Cologne after being placed on a wheel and dismembered with red-hot pincers (below, a series of 16th-century wood engravings depicting his capture, trial, and punishment). According to author Roland Villeneuve, the trial "revealed him as a true Massenmörder [mass murderer] who sodomized his daughter and his sister, violated his son before devouring his brain, and committed adultery with countless married women. Thirteen murders were

But this enormous fear was conveyed only through rumors, leaving no trace on the official register. It was not until the first decades of the 18th century that reports and accounts of eyewitnesses were gathered into written form, giving substance to what still passed largely as simple superstition.

confidently assigned to him, of children, shepherdesses, and pregnant women...."

Well into the 18th century, when, in the Age of Enlightenment, reason reigned triumphant, most superstitions took a battering. The cult of vampirism, however, literally exploded. The phenomenon assumed the dimensions of a true collective psychosis, affecting entire regions and arousing the interest of the highest civil, military, and religious authorities.

CHAPTER III
THE GOLDEN AGE OF VAMPIRISM

Epidemics of the bubonic plague (opposite, a view of Marseilles during the outbreak of 1720–3 by French painter Michel Serre) were sometimes attributed to supernatural causes. In eastern Europe, the vampire was often held to be the guilty party. Left: A 19th-century illustration of a vampire bat.

Visum et Repertum

An Explosion of Vampirism in the First Half of the 18th Century

At the time of the outbreak of the plague that ravaged eastern Prussia in 1710, the Austrian authorities then in control of the region had begun to carry out systematic investigations of the cases of vampirism brought to their attention, once going so far as to open all the tombs in a cemetery in order to catch the vampires that were supposedly responsible for the calamity.

The two most spectacular cases from this period are that of a Hungarian peasant named Peter Plogojowitz, presumed to have become a vampire after his death in 1725 and to have caused the death of eight people in the tiny village of Kisilova; and that of Arnold Paole, a peasant who, after dying from a fall from a haywagon around 1726, also turned into a vampire and was believed to have destroyed much of the human and animal populations of the Serbian village of Medvegia. The story of Plogojowitz was the subject of an official report that contained the first use of the term *vampire* (in German, spelled "vanpir").

The case of Arnold Paole caused a much bigger stir, starting with an official investigation

The plague epidemic suffered by the citizens of Marseilles in 1720–3 caused a great many casualties. In Serbia at around the same time raged a bovine plague, which was often fatal for humans. As soon as there was a certain number of suspicious deaths in a village, the cause was ascribed to a revenant. Intrigued by these superstitions, officials of the Austrian occupying regime called for investigations by doctors. The manuscript, a portion of which is reproduced above, was written by Johann Flückinger in December 1731. Published in April 1732 and reproduced and discussed in numerous publications, Flückinger's report helped to spread fear of the vampire throughout Europe. Left and opposite above: Details of the painting on the previous page.

that began in December 1731. The police report, entitled *Visum et Repertum* (Seen and Discovered), was written by an Austrian military doctor named Johann Flückinger and was countersigned by numerous military officers as well as other doctors. The report was sent to the Austrian council of war in Belgrade, the Serbian capital. Published in 1732 and reprinted many times, *Visum et Repertum* excited intense curiosity among the Western ruling class. The Austrian Emperor Charles VI (1685–1740) is reported to have closely followed the affair of Plogojowitz, and the French King Louis XV (1710–74) asked his advisor and

The nomadic peoples of central Europe, known generally as Bohemians or gypsies, contributed to both the spread and the enrichment of the vampire legend. Those living in Serbia, Bohemia, and Hungary, in particular, had an entire anthology concerning the different ways to identify and fight vampires—which did not prevent the native populations from suspecting the gypsies of entertaining close ties with the devil. Left: A 17th-century engraving of a gypsy encampment.

French ambassador to Austria, the Duc de Richelieu, for a detailed report on the official findings of the investigation. All in all, Plogojowitz and Paole caused a great deal of ink to flow in Europe. *Le Glaneur,* a Franco-Dutch periodical that was popular at Versailles, the court of Louis XV, presented the case of Arnold Paole in great detail in its issue of 3 March 1732. The word *vampire,* in this case spelled "vampyre," was here used in French for the first time. The same year, an article in the *London Journal* of 11 March 1732 introduced the word *vampire* into the English language.

Discourses of Doctors, Clerics, and Philosophers

These two and other similar affairs inspired an entire series of tracts and dissertations on the subject of vampirism and provoked innumerable discussions and controversies in literary circles and at universities. Until

The article about Arnold Paole in the 3 March 1732 issue of *Le Glaneur* created such a stir that the review took up the subject again in its issue of 17 March: "Some have flatly denied this prodigy; others have made it…one of their principal articles of belief: two extremes equally blameworthy, and which proceed from a shameful ignorance of the simplest effects of nature. The matter well deserves clarification, and we will not omit to offer posthaste the opinions of several clever physicians on the vampire."

this time, stories about supposed manifestations of vampirism came from an oral tradition fed by accounts transmitted from generation to generation as well as by rumors or simple gossip. In the 18th century, ostensibly in a show of the triumph of reason over superstition, all these stories were recorded, filed, and analyzed in learned works written mostly by scholars, doctors, and ecclesiastics of some renown.

An early tract, *Dissertatio Historica-Philosophica de Masticatione Mortuorum* (Historical and Philosophical Dissertation on the Chewing Dead), written by Philip Rohr (Leipzig, 1679), tried to explain the phenomenon

The fact that corpses could be found in their coffins without any cadaveric rigidity and spotted with blood several days after interment might indicate that the unfortunates were buried alive, placed in the coffin while in a comatose state mistaken for death, as illustrated in this early 19th-century painting by the Belgian artist Antoine-Joseph Wiertz.

of dead people who, apparently as a result of demonic possession, chewed in their tombs. The book aroused a lively controversy in the 18th century between those who accepted Rohr's supernatural explanation and those who rejected it in the name of reason, blaming the reported "facts" on superstition and ignorance.

In his celebrated tract *De Masticatione Mortuorum in Tumulis Liber* (Book of the Chewing Dead in Their Tombs), published in Leipzig in 1728, Michael Ranft refuted Rohr's hypotheses, asserting that even if the dead could act on the living, they could not in any case appear in tangible form, and that the devil did not have the power to enter the bodies of the dead. Among the many tracts that came out after the affair of Arnold Paole, two more German publications are worth mentioning because of their wide circulation: *Dissertatio Physica de Cadaveribus Sanguisugis* (Treatise on the Physical Nature of the Bloodsucking Corpse) by Johann Christian Stock (Jena, 1732) and *Dissertatio de Vampiris Serviensibus* (Treatise on Enslaved Vampires) by Johann Heinrich

DISSERTATIO HISTORICO-PHILOSOPHICA *De* MASTICATIONE MORTUORUM,

Zopft (Halle, 1733). According to these two authors, vampires were in reality dreams inspired by the devil.

The Church Involuntarily Recognized Vampirism

Faced with this avalanche of "scientific" tracts, the Church could not stay silent. One of the most famous works of the period was *Traité sur les Revenants en Corps, les Excommuniés, les Oupires ou Vampires, Broucolaques de Hongrie, de Moravie, etc.* (Treatise on the Returned in

In keeping with the rational spirit of the Age of Enlightenment, its thinkers, writers, and artists cast doubt on the supposed accomplishments of the devil and his associates, such as those pictured in the engraving above.

E Body, the Excommunicated, Vampires, Vrykolakas of Hungary, Moravia, etc.), by Dom Augustin Calmet (1672–1757), a French Benedictine monk who was well known for his expositions of the Bible. The exhaustive tract was published in two volumes in Paris in 1746. Wishing to confute the belief in vampires, Dom Calmet collected an impressive number of accounts of vampirism, and his book, although anecdotal and sometimes naive in tone, is of great interest to historians, sociologists, and anthropologists.

Calmet and other high-placed members of the clergy, in their attempts to make the Church's point of view known, inadvertently conferred on vampirism what amounted to official recognition. Such is the case with both Giuseppe Davanzati, archbishop of Florence, in his *Dissertatione Sopra*

Dom Calmet (below), in his famous tract, claimed to have completely laid to rest the controversial subject of vampirism.

i Vampiri (Dissertation on Vampires; Naples, 1744) and Pope Benedict XIV, Prospero Lambertini (1675–1758), who, in the process of refuting the existence of vampires, devoted several pages to them in Book IV of the second edition of his voluminous *De Servorum Dei Beatificatione et de Beatorum Canonizatione* (On the Beatification of the Servants of God and on the Canonization of the Beatified; Rome, 1749).

In France, the authors of the work that perhaps best exemplifies the main precepts of the Enlightenment— namely, skepticism and rationalism—the *Encyclopédie,* led by Denis Diderot (1713–84) and Jean Le Rond d'Alembert (1717–83), were alarmed by all the brouhaha surrounding vampires. One of the encyclopedia's contributors, the satirist Voltaire (1694–1778), gave vent to his indignation in his *Dictionnaire Philosophique.* Another, philosopher Jean-Jacques Rousseau (1712–78), castigated the belief in vampires in a letter he wrote to the

"It is above all up to you, as archbishop, to root up these super-stitions. In going to the source, you will discover that there might be some priests who spread them around in order to get the people to pay them for exorcisms and masses. I expressly enjoin you to suspend, without delay, those who would be capable of such a betrayal of trust; and I beg you to rest assured that it is only the living that are in the wrong in this matter.**"**

Pope Benedict XIV
letter to an archbishop
1756

archbishop of Paris. Both demanded to know how such a superstition could develop in the flowering of the Age of Enlightenment.

The advantages of all these tracts on vampirism in western Europe were that they made known to the public at large a group of beliefs that previously only a few travelers or diplomats had heard of and that they made the word *vampire* a generic term recognized by all. Before this, many different terms had been used to designate revenant bloodsuckers, but starting in 1732—that is, with the affair of Arnold Paole—*vampire,* in various spellings (vampyr, vampyre, wampire, etc.), or its Latin equivalent, *vampirus,* was systematically employed.

"You will find stories of vampires in the *Lettres Juives* [Jewish Letters; 1738] of [the Marquis] d'Argens [writer Jean-Baptiste de Boyer], whom the Jesuits…have accused of believing nothing. It should be observed how they triumph in the history of the vampire…; how they thanked God and the virgin for having at last converted this poor d'Argens…. Behold, said they, this famous unbeliever, who dared to throw doubts on the appearance of the angel to the holy virgin; on the star which conducted the magi; on the cure of the possessed; on the immersion of two thousand swine in a lake; on an eclipse of the sun at the full moon; on the resurrection of the dead who walked in Jerusalem; his heart is softened, his mind is enlightened: He believes in vampires."

Voltaire, *Philosophical Dictionary,* 1852

Bats of the suborders *Diphylla ecaudata, Desmodus rotundus,* and *Diaemus youngi* (above), found only in Central or South America, attack bovines and, very rarely, humans in their sleep. Although they can absorb only six tenths of a cubic inch of blood a day, their bite is dangerous because their saliva contains an anticoagulant, and they can spread infectious diseases such as the bubonic plague. The European and North American bat is harmless but has always aroused fright and repulsion.

An alternate manifestation of the vampire is depicted above left, in a 1935 illustration of a Romanian folk tale.

Notable Features of the Vampire

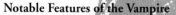

Beginning in the 18th century, the three characteristics that give the vampire its specific nature were finally united. First, the vampire is a revenant, or "one that returns in body," and not a filmy ghost or demon. Second, it leaves its tomb at night to suck the blood of mortals in order to prolong its posthumous existence. And third, its victims become vampires after their own deaths.

Ever since the release of the first screen adaptation of the Dracula story, movies have presented a somewhat distorted idea of the legendary vampire, tending to grossly exaggerate some aspects while minimizing others. The inability to register an image in the mirror, for example, is not a universal vampire trait. This particular belief emerges only from some regions of Germanic culture, where the vampire is similarly deprived of a shadow—the reflection and shadow in this instance symbolizing the soul that the revenant was thought to have lost. The overdeveloped teeth so dear to filmmakers are reminiscent of the werewolf's fangs but are an attribute that seems to have been made from whole cloth by the literature of fantasy. In general, the vampire does not bite its victims; it prefers to get blood by sucking the skin's pores.

Movies are also responsible for making the bat the semiobligatory emblem of the vampire. This is almost certainly attributable to the French naturalist Count Georges-Louis Leclerc de Buffon, who in 1760 gave the name vampire to Central and South American bats that suck the blood of cattle and other domesticated animals. In truth, the legendary vampire can transform itself into all sorts of animals, including spiders and butterflies, as well as fog or a piece of straw.

Another popular conception is that garlic is a useful prophylactic against the vampire. This particular belief, however, is specific to Romania. On the other hand, it is true that the vampire can go out only at night and must return to its tomb before the cock crows. It fears holy water—since sacred water is the source of life—as well as the consecrated wafer and the symbol of the cross. Finally, a stake plunged into a vampire's heart is in fact the best way to end its sacrilegious existence; but, cinematic assertions notwithstanding, this condition might not in itself suffice.

How Can One Identify a Vampire?

The 18th-century tracts on vampirism, added to 19th-century research, have permitted the major characteristics of this mythology to be made manifest. There are many

The garlic peddler, a popular character, could not fail to evoke the probable existence of vampires, against which his wares might prove a precious aid.

variations among European countries. Generally speaking, the vampire is a corpse that, even after several weeks' interment, has not decomposed in its tomb. Another broadly accepted peculiarity is that its hair is abnormally developed: A vampire's bushy eyebrows are joined together, and it has hairs on the palms of its hands. Romanian vampires sometimes have short tails covered with hair that might swell in the heat and are believed to give them their supernatural powers.

Other common beliefs about vampires include methods of detection. During outbreaks of vampirism, in order to identify the guilty party, an adolescent virgin was made to ride a virgin horse (either entirely black or entirely white) the length of the cemetery. At the tomb of the presumed vampire, the horse would rear. Another proof was the presence of tiny holes in the earth near the tomb. It was thought that the vampire, taking on the guise of fog, could leave the tomb through these holes. Persons born of the union of a vampire and a mortal were believed to have the gift of infallibly spotting vampires. These people were called *vampiritch* or *vampirovitch* in Serbia, *dhampires* in Bohemia and Hungary.

How Does One Become a Vampire?

In theory, everyone is susceptible to becoming a vampire after death, but some—such as the excommunicated, suicides, victims of violent death,

Pincers, a wooden mallet, and a sharply pointed stake form part of the traditional paraphernalia of the vampire hunter.

Professor Van Helsing, in Bram Stoker's *Dracula*, always carried these instruments in his doctor's bag. These illustrations are from the *Encyclopédie*.

witches, the stillborn, and anyone who has not had a Christian burial—are more vulnerable than others. Some people were thought to be predisposed to this deadly fate because of congenital peculiarities, such as being born with teeth, being born with a caul (a piece of the amniotic membrane or placenta that can cover the cranium at birth), having very dark eyes or very clear blue eyes, and having red hair or spots on the body.

When such people died, the precautions taken between the time a person was laid in the coffin through the interment were redoubled. In Romania, either a nail

Second to the cross, the cloves and flowers of garlic are said to provide the best protection against the vampire, which cannot abide the smell. In many countries, garlic has the reputation of keeping away all evil spirits. Pliny the Elder, a Roman scholar of the 1st century AD, reported that garlic offered protection from snakes and helped prevent madness.

was driven into the corpse's forehead or the body was pierced with needles or smeared with the fat of a pig killed on Saint Ignatius's Day. To prevent the soul of the alleged vampire from rejoining its body, one would place in its mouth a special object (in Romania, a clove of garlic; in Greece, a consecrated piece of bread; in Saxony, a lemon). To prevent the corpse from leaving its tomb, it was nailed to the bottom of the coffin. In Sudetenland (now part of the Czech Republic), the corpse of a suspected vampire was rolled up in a sort of stocking: Each year, the vampire would have to undo one stitch. In Russia,

In Christian Europe, vampirism was often considered a divine punishment. Blasphemers—such as these portrayed in an 18th-century engraving playing games on a tomb instead of attending the religious service—would have been especially prone to this curse.

people put poppy seeds in the coffin for the vampire to count every night or placed poppy seeds or briar spines on all the roads leading to the cemetery for the vampire to gather one by one. In Serbia, a cross painted with tar on the doors and windows protected a house from the vampire's attack. In Romania, strings of garlic were hung in every room, and garlic was rubbed on the doors, windows, chimneys, and keyholes.

The "Great Reparation," or the Death of the Vampire

Superstition dictated that to get rid of a vampire once and for all, the only thing to do was to pierce the heart with a wooden stake. The Russians used aspen, the wood that was used for Christ's cross, while other countries preferred the wood of the hawthorn shrub, in reference to Christ's crown of thorns. In Dalmatia and Albania, regions on the coast of the Adriatic, a dagger previously blessed by a priest was the weapon of choice. The execution, referred to in Romania as the "great reparation," had to transpire at the first light of dawn, and the officiating party had to drive in the stake with a single blow or risk the vampire's revival. If the body did not crumble into dust, its head had to be decapitated with a gravedigger's spade and the rest of its body burned, the ashes either thrown to the winds or buried at a crossroads.

The End of a Belief?

Even while vampirism became one of the main subjects of conversation in universities and literary

In Romania, the best defense against evil spirits remained religion. Below: A rendering of a weathered wooden cross from Romania.

salons toward the end of the 18th century, particularly in Germany and France, the presumed supernatural events that had so thoroughly tormented spirits in the first three decades of the century were becoming rare. The positivist ideas of the Enlightenment —the belief in the empirical sciences and the conviction that true knowledge can be gained from observing natural phenomena—slowly made their way to the farthest reaches of the European continent, and, along with the passing of the great plague epidemics, the belief in vampires inevitably declined. Although new instances of vampirism cropped up in the 19th century, they no longer constituted a mass phenomenon, and the industrialization of Europe would gradually bring new ways of living and force out the old, together with their superstitions. Even so, in some pockets of the Carpathians, belief in vampires persists. The triumphant rationalism of the century of Enlightenment got the better of the legendary vampire, but it could not banish it from the imagination. On the contrary, the Romantic movement, a rebellion against the atmosphere of material positivism and an expression of nostalgia for a fascinating and magical past, lost no time in resuscitating the vampire through literature.

Following the many controversies surrounding the vampire at the beginning of the 18th century, philosophers and members of the clergy alike condemned this belief in the name of logic and common sense.

Catholic or Protestant, the Church in the Age of Enlightenment continued to affirm the existence of God, the devil, and the resurrection of the dead but refuted that of ghosts and vampires. This famous 1762 engraving by English satirist William Hogarth (opposite and details left) takes aim not at religion per se but at the credulity, fanaticism, and superstition of certain bigoted types.

Fantasy can come alive only when the beliefs of the past have been laid to rest; on the other hand, while one might staunchly deny believing in vampires, one may still fear them. At the end of the 18th century, although belief in the vampire was no longer current, it served as a source of inspiration for literature and the graphic arts. Starting in 1797, Francisco de Goya, famous painter of Spanish court life, began a series of etchings entitled *Los Caprichos* (The Caprices), populated by swarms of menacing monsters. But these creatures have no objective existence; they live within us, lurking in the depths of our subconscious, emerging as soon as our logical faculty nods off. This concept is reflected in the title of the print at left, one of the Caprices, *El Sueño de la Razon Produce Monstruos* (The Sleep of Reason Produces Monsters). People today find vampires frightening not because they exist but because they embody humanity's most hidden fears and desires.

"Within, stood a tall old man, clean shaven save for a long white moustache, and clad in black from head to foot, without a single speck of colour about him anywhere." In 1897, through the pen of Bram Stoker, the vampire returned in force. Entering the realm of literature, Dracula became incarnate on the ambiguous stage of the imaginary, where the border of reality is sometimes blurred by fog.

DRACULA

BY

BRAM STOKER

WESTMINSTER
ARCHIBALD CONSTABLE AND COMPANY
2 WHITEHALL GARDENS
1897

CHAPTER IV

THE REAWAKENING OF THE VAMPIRE

A nightmare, in the shape of two dreadful animals watching a beautiful woman sleep, is depicted in the painting opposite by Anglo-Swiss painter Henry Fuseli. At left, the title page of Bram Stoker's *Dracula*.

Bram Stoker's novel, undeniably the product of Victorian society, gave rise to a veritable modern myth that, while perpetuating the legendary substratum of the vampire, at the same time profoundly changed its meaning. Nevertheless, it should be emphasized that Dracula was not born suddenly and accidentally from the imagination of a single individual, but rather is the culmination of a literary convention that dates back over one hundred years.

The Triumph of Rational Thought

The industrial revolution that began to change the European landscape in the second half of the 18th century engendered a new world in which the witches, demons, and revenants of the past had no place. While, as we have seen, the vampire draws its roots from the furthest reaches of human history, it is one of the last creations of a collective European mind. Embodying age-old fears, this new-fashioned monster

The grim aspect of both the mining towns (below) and the miners (above, an 1814 portrayal) was typical of England in the early 19th century. In the name of progress, the country had become work-oriented and materialistic following the social upheaval caused by the industrial revolution.

was born at the dawn of an era of rationalism, in a rural
Europe populated by superstitious peasants. Analyzed,
dissected, even ridiculed by the encyclopedists of the
18th century, logically it should have vanished and
become a simple museum curio. Indeed, in the second
half of the 18th century, newspapers wrote little
about vampires, so much more dazzled were
they by the prodigies of scientific
progress and technology.

At the beginning of the 19th century, newspapers occasionally mentioned the odd Hungarian or Serbian village where people were still opening tombs to look for vampires, but such subjects appear to have held little interest for most readers, whose life-style had been thoroughly upset by the advent of, among other things, metallurgy, railroads, and gas lighting.

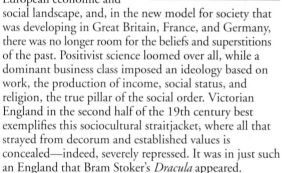

The industrial revolution quickly transformed the European economic and social landscape, and, in the new model for society that was developing in Great Britain, France, and Germany, there was no longer room for the beliefs and superstitions of the past. Positivist science loomed over all, while a dominant business class imposed an ideology based on work, the production of income, social status, and religion, the true pillar of the social order. Victorian England in the second half of the 19th century best exemplifies this sociocultural straitjacket, where all that strayed from decorum and established values is concealed—indeed, severely repressed. It was in just such an England that Bram Stoker's *Dracula* appeared.

Romanticism and the Rebirth of Vampirism

The Romanticism of the end of the 18th century might be viewed as, among other things, a reaction to both the positivism of the Enlightenment and the industrial revolution. The Romantics, following the highly emotional output of the *Sturm und Drang* (literally, storm and stress) literary movement in Germany and the gothic novel in England, rebelled against the prevailing rationalism and materialism, proclaiming the superiority of feeling and passion over cold, impersonal logic and asserting the primacy of the individual over the collective. They expressed nostalgia for times when people still believed

A land of contrasts, Victorian England was the setting for both the misery of slums crowded with the proletariat of mines and factories and the delightful gatherings of high society. Above left: Elegant settings such as this one captured by 19th-century French painter James Tissot were the inspiration for the aristocratic milieu in which Count Dracula operated.

in marvels and found inspiration in antiquity and the Middle Ages rather than the modern world.

At the turn of the century, the second generation of English Romantics displayed a lively interest in the supernatural. It was they who revived the legend of the vampire in their poetry. Theirs was, for the most part, a highly allegorical vampirism, which, following the great German models of the preceding generation, such as *Lenore* by Gottfried August Bürger (1773) and *Die Braut von Corinth* (The Bride of Corinth) by Johann von Goethe (1797), personified death in the guise of a young woman or young man come back from the beyond whose amorous embraces proved fatal. Here, vampirism becomes a sort of metaphor for the deadly passion so dear to the Romantics, thus constituting the first detour from the

British society of the Victorian era took a lively interest in new inventions without diminishing its traditional relish for the bizarre and the supernatural. Above: Dramatist, actor, and director Thomas William Robertson (1829–71) terrified his audiences by projecting spectral images onto a cloth using a lantern.

myth: The living dead described by Dom Calmet were in no way seducers, and the traditional legend was completely devoid of sexual connotations. Inspired by myths from antiquity or medieval ballads, the seductive vampires of Romantic poetry, such as Samuel Taylor Coleridge's *Christabel* (1816), John Keats's *La Belle Dame sans Merci* (1818) and *Lamia* (1820), were above all representations of the "femme fatale." It mattered little to their creators whether or not they sucked the blood of their victims. Their essential "advantage" was that they brought death and pleasure at the same time, and their "victims" were consenting adults. This brought a new strain of sado-masochism into the relationship between vampire and victim, a type of relationship between partners that persists in today's fantasy literature. The femme fatale presented in the guise of a vampire is a convention that remained current well beyond the Romantic period; the word *vamp,* meaning a seductive woman, came into popular usage in the early decades of the 20th century. In literature

Above: An illustration of Bürger's 1773 ballad *Lenore.* Right: A 19th-century drawing.

throughout Europe and America, the femme fatale qua vampire made numerous appearances in the 19th and 20th centuries. In 1866 French poet Charles-Pierre Baudelaire turned her into a putrid nymphomaniac in "Les Métamorphoses du Vampire." In prose, she would enjoy a long posterity as the delicious Clarimonde in French writer Théophile Gautier's "La Morte Amoureuse" (1857), and as the eponymous "Carmilla" (1871), Joseph Sheridan Le Fanu's seductive and mysterious heroine—not to mention the three captive beauties in Dracula's castle who make the heart of Stoker's protagonist, Jonathan Harker, beat fast.

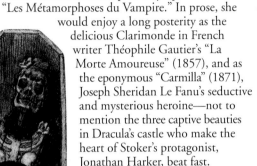

The Vampire Entered the World of Prose

Undoubtedly, the vampire would never have won over the general public if it had been restricted to the domain of poetry, and the character of Dracula as conceived by Stoker would never have materialized had it not been for its precursor Lord Ruthven, hero of *The Vampyre,* a novel by Englishman John William Polidori (1795–1821), who, almost by accident, introduced the vampire into prose literature. It all started in Geneva in June 1816. After an evening of relating ghost stories to one another, English Romantic poet Lord Byron (1788–1824) and his traveling companions (including fellow writers Percy Bysshe and Mary Wollstonecraft Shelley

While a dark Romanticism took hold of the graphic arts, John William Polidori (above) introduced the vampire into prose literature. Unhappily for him, his tale, *The Vampyre,* was credited to his former employer, Lord Byron. The first masterpiece of the short story genre, "La Morte Amoureuse" (The Dead Lover) by Théophile Gautier, tells the story of an impossible love between the young priest Romuald and the beautiful vampire Clarimonde (following pages).

MORT

and Byron's personal secretary and physician, Dr. John Polidori) decided to hold a competition in which they would create their own tales of suspense. Lord Byron undertook the writing of a novel with a vampire hero named Darvell. The work went unfinished (unlike Mary Shelley's, whose completed story, *Frankenstein,* remains one of the all-time best novels of terror), but Byron confided the plot to Polidori. The latter, who detested his employer, eventually left his employ and Switzerland, returning to England in 1817. Soon thereafter Polidori began his own novel, inspired by Byron's unfinished story but using different names for the characters. The vampire Darvell became Lord Ruthven, a cynical and debauched seducer who strangely resembled Byron. The tale was published in England in April 1819 in the *New Monthly Magazine* and fraudulently credited by the magazine's publisher to Byron. This illustrious patronage, which the unhappy Polidori had thought safely behind him, turned out to guarantee many reprintings of the novel, its translation into French, and its adaptation for the theater as a melodrama—first by Charles Nodier in 1820 and then by Alexandre Dumas (the elder) in 1852. Thanks to Byron's notoriety,

Today, French writer Charles Nodier (1780–1844) is better known for his tales of fantasy than for his stage adaptation of Polidori's *The Vampyre.* The engraving shown below, from an 1846 edition of Nodier's *Contes* (Tales), shows a nightmare in the guise of a strige.

LE
MÉ

VAMPIRE

ODRAME EN TROIS ACTES,

VEC UN PROLOGUE,

Polidori's tale launched the vampire literary vogue in Europe and engendered many imitations.

Polidori's book is of prime importance in the history of the vampire in literature, as it introduced the character to the general public and created the convention of the aristocratic vampire—a creature at once arrogant and seductive—of which Stoker's Dracula is an illustrious embodiment.

Taken with Nodier's play (above, an advertisement for it), French author Alexandre Dumas wrote his own version: *Vampire*, in five acts, performed for the first time in 1851 (top, a scene from the drama).

The Craze for Tales of Horror

The wave of popularity created by the vampire's appearance onstage and in popular literature crested after 1850. Due to their repetitive nature, the texts became more sporadic, and their quality diminished: Over most of Europe, the vampire died by boring its public. But not in Victorian England, which revealed an increasingly marked affinity for fantasy and horror.

The British public's infatuation with the supernatural and the macabre was nothing new: It belonged to a national tradition going back to the beginning of the country's history. Great Britain was always a land of ghosts, a place where frightening stories were beloved. The industrial revolution indirectly reinforced that tradition. In the materialistic and prudish Victorian society that preached the values of work, money, and religion, fantasy appeared to many as a marvelous means of escape. Reading terrifying stories in which the proper

On this page are three illustrations from the 1847 *Varney the Vampyre*—with 868 pages and 220 chapters, the longest novel written on the subject. *Varney,* successively attributed to two obscure novelists, Thomas Peckett Prest and James Malcom Rymer, served as a prototype for the type of vampire story that emphasized horror and terror. After having assumed various identities and undergone all sorts of adventures, the protagonist, Sir Francis Varney, weary of his long existence, throws himself into Mount Vesuvius. A picaresque narrative rife with reversals, it keeps the reader in suspense right up to the climax.

order of things is pooh-poohed and the established morality is questioned became a kind of collective outlet, as witnessed by the success of "penny dreadfuls," magazines that disseminated in the form of endless serials such heinous stories as *Varney the Vampyre*, a saga later published anonymously in book form (1847).

Carmilla, Dracula's Ancestor

In the last decades of the 19th century, the rage for stories about revenants had penetrated every level of Victorian society, and even the most celebrated writers, including Charles Dickens (1812–70) and Edward George Bulwer-Lytton (1803–73), did not hesitate to add their contributions—Dickens with "The Haunted House" and Lytton with "The Haunted and the Haunters," both in 1859. The hypocrisy of the system was such that it was perfectly permissible to write the most horrific and squalid story as long as the language was covert and morality triumphed in the end, conditions that got it through the censor's net.

This was the setting for the appearance of the story "Carmilla" in 1871 by Irishman Joseph Sheridan Le Fanu (1814–73), who renewed the grand tradition of vampirism and anticipated Bram Stoker's *Dracula*. Returning to the creature's sources—the plot of this

The short story "Carmilla," by Joseph Sheridan Le Fanu is considered one of the masterpieces of the genre. Above, Carmilla makes a nighttime visit to one of her victims. Carmilla, more sensual than Gautier's Clarimonde, chooses only victims of her own gender. The ambiguity of the relations between the vampire countess and the narrator Laura, and the dreamlike nature of the narrative, create a disturbing and phantasmagoric atmosphere. On the following pages, the theme of the female vampire is illustrated by canvases by the Norwegian expressionist painter Edvard Munch (p. 80 and p. 81 above) and Polish sculptor-painter Boleslas Biegas (p. 81 below, left and right).

novella unfolds in Styria (in central Austria), the vampires' location of choice, and the principal character, Countess Mircalla von Karnstein, alias Carmilla, is clearly inspired by Countess Báthory—Le Fanu nimbly exploits the sexual dimension of vampirism: His eponymous heroine is a sensual creature, perceived through the lens of Victorian society as the incarnation of absolute evil. The story is simultaneously edifying, with evil decisively defeated with the aid of God, and scandalous —in a land that considered homosexuality a crime, it describes rather equivocal relations between the female vampire and its female "victim."

DRACULA

CHANSON MYSTERIEUSE

For the Piano

Born near Dublin on 8 November 1847, Bram Stoker (above right) was destined for a career in government, but a meeting with the actor Henry Irving (1838–1905, above left) in 1876 changed his course. Hired by Irving as stage director of the Lyceum Theatre, Stoker soon moved to London. His final years were shadowed by the failure of the Lyceum in 1903 and Irving's death two years later. A stage version of *Dracula* by Stoker (program opposite) played only once at the Lyceum; Irving thought it "dreadful." Left: Detail of sheet-music for a piano piece written in 1927.

Le Fanu thus managed to satisfy the perverse cravings of his readers while heeding the strictures of official morality. Bram Stoker would follow his example.

Dracula: The Apogee of the Vampire in the 19th Century

The publication of *Dracula* in 1897 marked a true turning point in the history of vampirism in literature, constituting simultaneously a renewal of the gothic genre of the 18th century, a return to the orthodox legend of the vampire, and, most important, the founding of a myth for modern times.

The author himself must have been taken aback by his book's success. Bram Stoker was not a professional writer. Stage manager of London's Lyceum Theatre, which was directed by his friend Henry Irving, Stoker regarded writing as a hobby, and it was not until after the theater failed in 1903 that he turned to full-time writing to earn his living. Infatuated with fantasy literature at an early age, Stoker had read the great classics of vampire literature, namely, *The Vampyre, Varney the Vampyre,* and "Carmilla," as well as *A Mysterious Stranger,* a novel translated from German and published anonymously in

"The master of the Carpathian castle seemed to resemble the ruling hand of the Lyceum Theatre in many regards. Irving had a reputation for being excessively demanding, tyrannical, egotistic, living only for the theater, all of which undoubtedly worked a literal 'psychological vampirism' on the person of Stoker.**"**

Alain Pozzuoli,
Bram Stoker, Prince des Ténèbres (Prince of Darkness), 1989

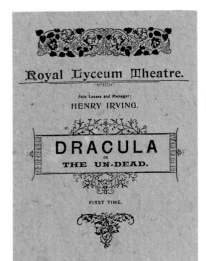

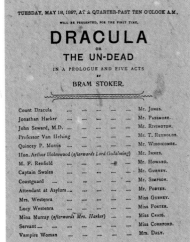

1860. Eager to write his own vampire story, he began seriously to examine vampirism and the Transylvanian legends, studying in particular *The Land Beyond the Forest* (1888), a travel and culture guide to Transylvania written by Emily Gerard.

A member of a cult group, the esoteric Order of the Golden Dawn, he immersed himself in the occult and black magic. The determining factor in the establishment of his protagonist was his acquaintance with Arminius Vambery, a professor of eastern languages at the University of Budapest, who was well versed in the history and folklore of central Europe. During a visit to London,

"Little by little, Dracula begins to take shape, slowly, patiently. But Stoker is a perfectionist, a lover of detail, and before unleashing his terrifying creature of the night on the world of the living, he must ground him in the actual historical and geographic context."
Alain Pozzuoli
Bram Stoker, Prince des Ténèbres, 1989

Vambery told Stoker the story of the real-life Dracula, the terrible Vlad Tepes, and the writer, taken by the exotic sound of the name, decided to use it for the lead character of his novel. *Dracula* appeared in 1897, and the first chapter, which the author had decided to leave out, was published separately by Stoker's widow in 1914 in the form of a novella entitled *Dracula's Guest*. It includes a female character, the Countess Dolingen of Gratz, inspired no doubt by Carmilla.

Jonathan Harker Sets Out for Transylvania

As the plot of the novel is known mostly through the somewhat distorted movie version, it is necessary to provide a brief synopsis of the original. Jonathan Harker, a young legal assistant, is sent to Transylvania to conduct a business transaction with a certain Count Dracula, who wishes to buy property in

In Stoker's novel, the most important character besides Dracula is Professor Van Helsing, played by Edward Van Sloan in Tod Browning's famous 1931 film (at left, opening the casket that holds the vampire). Dracula's antithesis, the wise patriarch Van Helsing embodies good, which must in the end triumph over the forces of evil. If some interpreters of the novel claim to see in Dracula a representation of Stoker's father, authoritarian and uncompromising, one might regard Van Helsing, whose first name—like that of Stoker and his father—is Abraham, as Stoker's ideal father, just and benevolent.

Left: Dracula attacks a young woman who has foolishly left the window of her bedroom open while she sleeps. The winged monster who seems to be watching over the scene with satisfaction makes the demonic nature of the vampire, Satan's hench-man, absolutely clear.

England. As the plot unravels (the novel is presented as an actual record, with letters, diaries, and so on), Harker discovers the terrible secret of his host: Count Dracula is a member of the living dead, a vampire who emerges from its coffin at night to slake its thirst for human blood. The brave young man follows the trail of his host's crimes and thus begins the first stages of the struggle between good and evil that ultimately ensnares him. Early in the game, evil triumphs, Dracula choosing Lucy, a friend of Harker's fiancée, Mina, for his victim. The luckless Lucy dies, drained of her blood. But in the end the forces of good gain the upper hand: Harker, Mina,

Professor Van Helsing, and the American Quincey Morris conquer the vampire. As Morris's bowie knife pierces his heart, Dracula crumbles into dust, and Mina is saved from his evil spell.

The convincingly journalistic form of the book allows the reader to follow the hero step by step as he first discovers the horror and then in his fight against evil. As a novel, *Dracula* is unique in its genre. It restores the atmosphere of gothic novels—with its evocation of a partially ruined medieval castle, whose subterranean crypts conceal horrifying mysteries—yet it is set in the modern world at the end of the 19th century. Part of the novel takes place in London, and the latest medical discoveries (notably those in the new field of psychiatry) are constantly evoked. It is also the first book of its kind to exude the odor of authenticity:

Tod Browning's film version of *Dracula* has images of immense beauty, particularly in the sequences that take place at Dracula's castle. The movie follows Stoker's plot fairly closely, except that some of the secondary characters were inverted and their names slightly changed. For example, Lucy Westenra becomes Lucy Weston; Mina is no longer the wife of Jonathan Harker (who is named John in the movie) but of Dr. Holmwood; and it is not Harker who goes to the castle to conduct the real-estate transaction but the demented Renfield, wonderfully acted by Dwight Frye. Bela Lugosi (Dracula), left, gets ready to bite the jugular of Helen Chandler (Mina).

The author spent much time at the British Museum researching not only vampirism but also the history, geography, manners, customs, and folklore of Transylvania. Unlike his predecessors, Stoker's hero displays all the characteristics of the traditional vampire: He has no reflection, he cowers from garlic and the symbols of Christianity, he can assume at will the guise of an animal, he revives only at night, and he feeds exclusively on blood. In fact, despite some dull spots and awkwardness, *Dracula* could be considered a masterpiece of fantasy literature. Constantly reprinted and translated into the world's major languages, it has inspired a prolific literature and created a mythic figure which the 20th century was to give a particular emphasis.

THE WORLD'S MOST HORRIBLE THRILLER

DRACULA
by
Bram Stoker

Dracula: **Erotic or Edifying?**

From the day of its debut, *Dracula* enjoyed unquestionably widespread success, although, given the book's notoriety, it was not as huge a triumph as one might imagine. The British press on the whole received it favorably: The *Pall Mall Gazette* called it "excellent," and the *Daily Mail* compared it, not without exaggeration, to those great masterpieces of English literature *Wuthering Heights* (1847) by Emily Brontë and *The Fall of the House of Usher* (1839–40) by Edgar Allan Poe. *Dracula* possessed all the requisite qualities to please a Victorian public avid for terrifying tales of the supernatural, yet

As this publicity headline (above left) indicates, the notoriety of *Dracula* made its way around the globe. This classic of horror literature can hold its own in comparison with Mary Shelley's *Frankenstein* (1818), an earlier classic of the same genre.

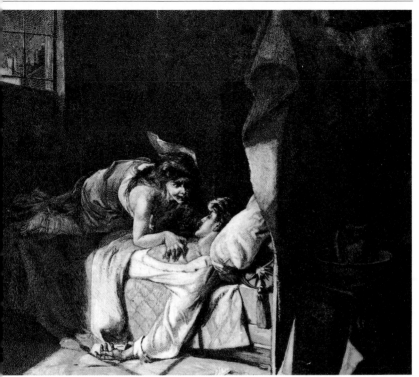

satisfied the strict moral code by showing the triumph of virtue over vice. Besides, the satanic character of Dracula, the manifestation of evil in all its forms, came from a faraway land on the Continent to upset the harmonious order of British society, which pleased the latently xenophobic Victorians. The novel's turgid sensuality, transparently implicit in certain passages, is the author's wink to a readership that, without openly admitting it, was suffocating in the straitjacket of official decorum and morality. For the reader who saw the text objectively, this book falsely labeled edifying turned out to be extremely erotic as well as subversive, to the extent that the count dominates the other characters, mere mediocre representatives of Victorian society, both physically and mentally.

At the time *Dracula* appeared, near the turn of the century, the Victorian mentality was not the only mind-set. The ideas of the "decadents" were very much in vogue throughout Europe. Intellectual circles acquired a marked taste for the morbid, the exotic, and the shocking. Above: *The Female Vampire,* an engraving after a painting made by German artist Max Kahn around 1895.

The Birth of the Myth in the 20th Century

While *Dracula* was welcomed from the moment of its publication, it did not attain the dimensions of myth in the author's lifetime. Dracula was much less popular than Sherlock Holmes, and Bram Stoker was not nearly as famous as Sir Arthur Conan Doyle, Holmes's creator, who received hundreds of letters from his readers. It was first the stage and then the screen that took Stoker's *Dracula* to mythic heights.

In June 1924, twelve years after Stoker's death, *Dracula* appeared onstage for the first time at Derby, England, in the form of an adaptation by Hamilton Deane. For the occasion, the hero dressed in the costume that would invariably form part of the modern vampire's representation: evening dress and black cape. The play, revived in London in June 1927, was so successful that it crossed the Atlantic in September of the same year to become a hit on Broadway, where the role of the count was played by a Hungarian actor named Bela Lugosi. Lugosi's authoritative embodiment of the character in a film made four years later assured Dracula's entry into legend.

The first actor to portray Dracula onscreen, in Murnau's *Nosferatu* (1922), Max Schreck (above) created a very different character from the one described in the novel. While Stoker's Dracula was tall and majestic, Murnau's was small, frail, and bald, with a demonic persona. As Murnau had not received permission from Stoker's widow to adapt the novel to the screen, he had to change the title and the names of the characters. The vampire, for instance, became Count Orlok, alias Nosferatu. Notwithstanding, the Berlin production company was forced to destroy the film, although a few copies, fortunately, were preserved.

The first talking film adapted from Stoker's novel, Tod Browning's *Dracula* (1931, with Bela Lugosi in the starring role), is traditionally regarded as the beginning of the modern myth. In reality, however, it was preceded by F. W. Murnau's silent *Nosferatu,* a German expressionist masterpiece whose premiere in 1922 went almost unnoticed. Tod Browning's film also overshadowed another masterpiece of world cinema, the wonderful *Vampyr,* loosely adapted from "Carmilla" by Danish filmmaker Carl Theodor Dreyer. Thus, the modern myth of Dracula was truly born in Hollywood in 1931.

The site and the time did not arise by accident. The United States was going

BLOODY TERROR TRANSYLVANIA
BELA LUGOSI
HELEN CHANDLER
TOD BROWNING ABRAHAM STOKER

After playing the role of Dracula on Broadway, where he had already appeared wearing evening dress (above) and his famous cape (left), Bela Lugosi took the lead in Tod Browning's film adaptation. While his impersonation also differed from Stoker's description (an old man with a long, white mustache), Lugosi had the required aristocratic demeanor and central European accent. The image of Dracula that Lugosi created became the standard, imitated the world over. After World War II, Lugosi's star faded, and he was reduced to playing Dracula in mediocre parodies. By his death in 1956 his public image was inseparable from the costume that had made his name.

Next to Bela Lugosi, the best-known interpreter of Dracula is the British actor Christopher Lee, seen here (left) in Terence Fisher's *Dracula* (1958), the first color film of Stoker's novel. While the film, like its predecessors, took great liberties with the original action (the movie takes place in Germany, Harker dies in Dracula's castle, the parts of Mina and Lucy are reversed, and the demented Renfield is omitted), the leading actor much more closely approximates the novel's description of Dracula: a man of great height with thick eyebrows, aquiline nose, and an authoritarian and violent manner. In *Count Dracula* (1971), directed by Jesus Franco, the resemblance to the original was even more striking: Here, Christopher Lee portrayed an old man with white hair and a long mustache. Lee also borrowed the characteristics of the historic Dracula, Vlad Tepes, to whom he had a striking resemblance, judging from the portraits of the time.

through one of the blackest periods in its history. The stock market crash of 1929 had ruined millions of people. In the eyes of the American public, Dracula, more than any other screen monster, crystallized in his person all the hatred and anguish unleashed by the economic crisis. Again, a symbolic representation of the detested foreigner was made to bear responsibility for all of society's ills. Bela Lugosi's Hungarian accent, pale complexion, and sickly smile reinforced this identification.

In their turn, the movies gave rise to an outpouring of popular literature in the United States that lasted until the end of World War II. Dracula and his like, fitted with Slavic or German names, embodied Bolshevism and Nazism in the collective unconscious, resulting in an extraordinary deviation from the original myth.

The Internationalization of the Myth

In the 1950s, American popular culture found its way into every country outside of the Communist bloc. As an integral part of the "American way of life," the myth of Dracula was spread abroad. Vampire films were made in Italy, Spain,

Mexico, even the Philippines. Dracula himself changed his face: In 1958, in *Dracula,* directed by Terence Fisher, British actor Christopher Lee played the part earlier filled by Bela Lugosi. In later versions Lon Chaney and John Carradine would re-create the role. Physically very different from Lugosi, Lee immediately created a new image of the vampire count. Beneath the handsome features of a tall, fiftyish man with graying temples and a regal carriage, aristocratic distinction and bestiality appear by turns. Before this, Dracula had been fitted out with long, sharp canines revealed by lips grotesquely pulled back. Lee embodied Stoker's character in so many movies that in 1976, tired of the constraints of the part, he parodied himself in a French

comic film directed by Eduard Molinero, *Dracula, Père et Fils,* adapted from a novel by Claude Klotz entitled *Paris Vampire.* For an entire generation, Lee was identified so completely with his character that most of the actors who followed him in the role were often content simply to imitate him.

Fisher's *Dracula* returned the vampire to popularity. Since then, innumerable films have been made on the theme. In addition to those devoted to Dracula or similar characters were others inspired by "Carmilla" and Countess Báthory. A few of these escaped the common-place. Left, from top to bottom: Poster for the French version of Fisher's 1958 *Dracula*; a still from *Les Lèvres Rouges* (1971) directed by Harry Kummel, starring Delphine Seyrig as a modern-day Countess Báthory; a poster for Roger Vadim's *Et Mourir de Plaisir* (1960), with Annette Vadim (shown here with Elsa Martinelli) as Carmilla; a still from *The Fearless Vampire Killers* (1967), showing Roman Polanski about to drive a stake through Count Krolock's heart; and a scene from Werner Herzog's *Nosferatu the Vampyre* (1979), in which Klaus Kinski (Nosferatu) victimizes Bruno Ganz (Jonathan Harker).

1 Litre 12.50
½ litre............8.00
Le demi-setier....4.00

englisch
spoken

PAUL
COLIN

Vampirism is not always taken so seriously: left, a poster for a French comedy; below, a bat umbrella.

The year 1979 marked a clear turning point in the conception of Dracula's film image, thanks to two very different movies that broke from the conventional mold. The first, German director Werner Herzog's *Nosferatu the Vampyre,* in some ways represented a return to the source; the actor playing Nosferatu, Klaus Kinski, reused the makeup of Max Schreck, who had played the hero in Murnau's film: bald head, pointed ears, enormous incisors, and nightmarish face. The second, John Badham's *Dracula,* went in the opposite direction and featured a young and seductive vampire, played by Frank Langella, who possessed irresistible charm.

Dracula Today

It must be remembered that *Dracula* is not the only novel to have inspired vampire films. Le Fanu's "Carmilla" was many times translated to the screen, the best result

...ND VAMPIRELLA PRODUCES A VIAL OF THICK, DARK FLUID... THE SPECIAL SERUM THAT TAKEN ONCE EACH 24 HOURS KEEPS HER FROM BEING A HUNTRESS PREYING ON THE BLOOD OF MANKIND.

VAMPIRELLA...! I WAS DYING... Y-YOU...

perhaps being Roger Vadim's 1960 *Et Mourir de Plaisir* (And to Die of Pleasure). Countess Báthory also enjoyed considerable cinematic success, notably in the person of Delphine Seyrig, who lent her beautiful, enigmatic face to *Les Lèvres Rouges* (The Red Lips), directed by Harry Kummel (1971).

Contemporary films tend to look beyond the stereotypes of the genre, and the theme of the vampire has seen a revival in such films as *The Hunger* (1983) and *Near Dark* (1987), both of which offer completely updated images of the vampire.

Thanks to the movies, literature, television, and comic books, the myth has been kept alive, although its meaning changes with each new context. Today's vampire tends to be a secular creature that no longer shies from garlic or religious symbols. It has also lost most of its magical properties, its titles of nobility, and its castle in the Carpathians, preferring instead to mix with the crowds in modern cities. If it remains a bloodthirsty nocturnal predator, it might show a seductive side, or even a sympathetic aspect, placing it at the opposite end of the spectrum from both the vampires of legend and Bram Stoker's Dracula. But despite these profound changes, the modern vampire continues to embody—like the lamiae of antiquity and the living dead of Transylvania—all the fascination and anguish inspired in us by blood, the night, life, and death.

Cartoons and comic books have also appropriated the vampire. Dracula has become a transatlantic hero as popular as Tarzan or Batman. But he has found a strong rival in the person of Vampirella (left and below). In a comic book series begun in 1969 by Forrest J. Ackerman, Vampirella, like Superman, comes from another planet, Drakulon, and possesses supernatural powers. Substituting a synthetic substance for blood, Vampirella no longer poses a threat to humans. Overleaf: A modern Hungarian version of the famous count.

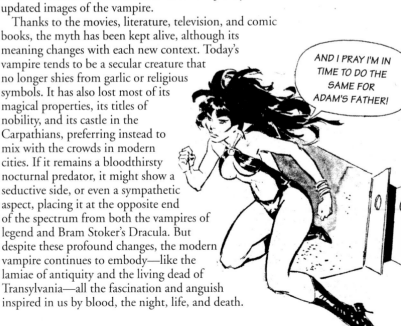

AND I PRAY I'M IN TIME TO DO THE SAME FOR ADAM'S FATHER!

DOCUMENTS

A Tyrant Named Dracula

"[Once upon a time] there was in the land of Muntenia [Walachia, southern Romania] a Greek Orthodox voivode, whose name in Romanian was Dracula, which means in our language 'the devil.' He was so wicked that his life was the image of his name."

Russian Chronicles

The punishments meted out by the historic Dracula, a 15th-century prince named Vlad Dracul Tepes, inspired horrifying chronicles. As can be seen from the following incidents, retold from authentic contemporary reports, Vlad held a very particular concept of the respect due his person as well as of justice in general.

A Lesson in Politeness

One day there came before him ambassadors from the Great Turk, and while they were being introduced to him, they bowed, as was their custom, but did not remove their head coverings. Then he asked them, "Why are you behaving thus? You are standing before a great sovereign and you insult me in this way?"

They responded, "Such is the custom of our sovereign and our land."

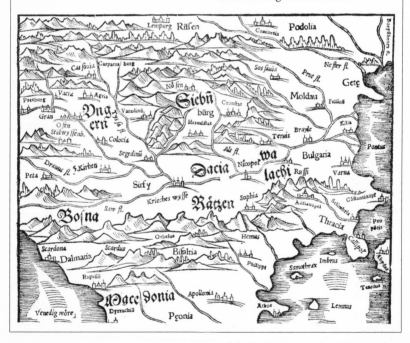

And Vlad told them, "Very well, I am going to strengthen you in your custom. Hold tight!" And he ordered their turbans fixed to their heads with small iron nails. He then let them go, with the words, "Go and tell your sovereign that even if he is used to accepting such humiliation from you, we have no such habitude. And that he not impose his customs on other sovereigns who want no part of them but that he keep them for himself."

How to Gain Paradise

One day Vlad had it broadcast throughout his land that all those who were old and sick, suffering from infirmities or poor, should come to him. And an enormous crowd of beggars and vagabonds gathered, in expectation of a grand act of charity. And he ordered that they be placed together in a magnificent mansion made for the occasion and that they be given all they wished to eat and drink. After having eaten their fill, they began to amuse themselves. Then Vlad himself paid them a visit and asked them, "What more do you require?"

And they replied in unison, "Our lord, only God and your greatness, of which he knows, as God will make it known to you."

He then said, "Would you like me to arrange it so that you no longer have any cares, and that you will lack nothing more in this world?"

And, expecting some great benefaction, all replied, "Yes, we so desire, our lord!" On hearing this, he ordered that the house be bolted and set on fire, and all perished in the flames. During this time, he said to his boyars [noblemen], "Know that I did that first of all so that they would no longer impose a burden on others and that there no longer be any poor people in my land, so that all should be rich. Secondly, I released them so that none of them should any longer suffer from poverty or infirmity in this world."

Virtue Rewarded

One day a foreign merchant from Hungary arrived in Dracula's city. Following regulations, he left his wagon in the street in front of the house in which he was to spend the night, leaving his merchandise in the vehicle. Someone having stolen 160 ducats of gold from the wagon, the merchant presented himself before Vlad to report the loss of his gold. Vlad said to him, "You may go in peace. Tonight, your gold will be returned." And he ordered that the thief be sought throughout the city while making it known that if the thief were not found, he would destroy the entire city. He ordered that the amount of gold lost be placed in the wagon during the night, but he added a coin. Awakening, the merchant found the gold, and after counting it twice, discovered an extra coin. He went to Vlad and told him, "Sire, I found the gold, but look, there's an extra coin that doesn't belong to me." Just then, the thief was brought in. And Vlad addressed the merchant, "Go in peace! If you hadn't mentioned that extra piece of gold, I was ready to impale you next to this thief."

Matei Cazacu
L'Histoire du Prince Dracula, en Europe Centrale et Orientale (History of Prince Dracula in Central and Eastern Europe)
1988

A 16th-century map showing the region now occupied by Romania and Bulgaria. The Transylvanian Alps appear in the center.

Vampirism Through the Centuries

Numerous accounts attesting to the existence of revenants, or the "walking dead," have been collected since as long ago as the 11th century, well before the term vampire *was invented.*

One of the earliest known cases of a revenant was referred to in the minutes of the proceedings of a church council held in 1304.

Then the bishop of Chartres began an account; he said, "Very recently, after the Council of Bourges, a knight of our diocese, excommunicated, was killed. Despite the pleas of his friends and relatives, I refused to give him absolution in order to strike fear into the hearts of others; he had, in effect, committed a grievous act of pillage. Under the escort of a priest he was buried, without my authorization, by soldiers near a certain Church of Saint Peter.

"Now, on the following morning, his body was thrown far outside the cemetery, nude on the earth. When the soldiers discovered him he was wearing

The Mourning of Laszlo Hunyadi, a late-19th-century painting by Viktor de Madarasz.

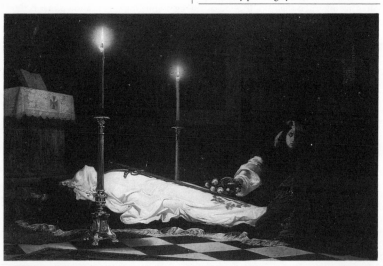

nothing but the shroud in which he was buried. Once more they buried his corpse, taking pains to close the tomb under an enormous weight of earth and rocks, but the next day they again saw the corpse flung out and the tomb intact.

"Five times they buried him; five times with the same fright they witnessed him thrown far away. Finally convinced by this terrifying phenomenon, they covered the body with earth far from the church's cemetery. Struck with terror, the heads of the army did not linger, as we would have wished, to make peace with us."

At that the Council responded, "What does that mean if not, before the eyes of men, the supreme arbiter confirms the authority of the Church, and that it is with all due justice that the excommunicated are denied Christian burial by the bishops? Such individuals in effect disown their faith in giving themselves to plunder instead of peace."

Minutes of the Council of 1304
(quoted in Tony Faivre
Les Vampires, 1962)

In addition to being a clergyman, Walter Map (c. 1140–c. 1209), appointed archdeacon of Oxford in 1197, was a writer and a wit. He related many stories of the living dead, including the following:

William Laudun, an English soldier, a man of great strength and proven courage, went to Gilbert Foliot, who was at that time Bishop of Hereford, but is now Bishop of London, and said to him, "My lord, I come to thee to ask for counsel. A certain Welsh malefactor recently died in my house, a man who professed to believe in nothing, and after an interval of four nights he has returned each night and has not failed on each occasion to summon forth severally and by name one of his fellow lodgers. As soon as they are called by him they sicken and within three days they die, so that now but a few are left."

The Bishop, who was greatly amazed, answered: "Perhaps power hath been given by the Lord to the evil angel of that accursed wretch so that he is able to rouse himself and walk abroad in his dead body. However, let the corpse be exhumed, and then do you cut through its neck sprinkling both the body and the grave throughout with holy water, and so rebury it."

This was acccordingly done, but none the less the survivors were tormented and attacked by the wandering spirit. Now it happened that on a certain night when only very few were left William himself was called three times by name. But he being bold and active and knowing who it was suddenly rushed out, brandishing his drawn sword.

The demon fled fast but he pursued it to the very grave, and as it lay therein he clave its head clean through from the neck. At that very hour, the persecution they endured from this demoniacal wanderer ceased, and since that time neither William himself nor any one of the others has suffered any harm therefrom.

Walter Map
De Nugis Curialium
(Courtiers' Triflings)
c. 1182–92
(quoted in Montague Summers
The Vampire in Europe, 1929)

Map's contemporary, historian William of Newburgh (1136–c.1198), describes a figure that in some respects resembles the modern vampire.

Some years ago there died the chaplain of a certain lady of high rank, and he was buried in that stately and magnificent monastery, the Abbey of Melrose. Unfortunately, this priest little respected the sacred vows of his holy order and he passed his days almost as if he were a layman.… And it is quite plain from what happened after his death that he was commonly held in very light esteem, and his guilt was most censurable, nay, even heinous. For several nights he made his way out of his grave and endeavoured to force an entrance into the cloister itself, but herein he failed and he was unable either to injure or even to alarm anybody at all, so great were the merits and the holiness of the good monks who lived there. After that he proceeded to wander further abroad, and suddenly he appeared in the chamber at the very bedside of the lady whose chaplain he had been and uttered the most piercing shrieks and heart-rending groans. When this had taken place more than once, she was almost distraught with fear, dreading that some terrible danger might happen to her, and summoning a senior of the brethren from the monastery she besought him with tears that they should offer special prayers on her behalf since she was tormented in a most extraordinary and unusual manner. When he had heard her story the monk calmed her anxiety… and…promised that before long a remedy should be found. As soon as he had returned to the monastery he

divulged his plan to a prudent and wise monk, and they decided that in company with two stout and brave-hearted young men, they would watch all night in that part of the graveyard where the unhappy priest had been buried.… Twelve o'clock had already struck, and yet there was no sign of this monster. Accordingly, three of the company withdrew for a while that they might warm themselves by the fire in a lodge near at hand…yet the monk who had requested the others to join him resolved not to relinquish his vigil. Now when he was left alone in this place, the Devil, thinking that he had found a fine opportunity to break down the pious man's courage and constancy, aroused from his grave that instrument of his.…

When the monk saw the monster close at hand realizing that he was all alone, he felt a thrill of horror; but in a moment his courage returned. He had no thought of flight, and as the horrible creature rushed at him with the most hideous yell, he firmly stood his ground, dealing it a terrific blow with a battle-axe which he held in his hand. When the dead man received this wound he groaned aloud with a terrible hollow noise, and swiftly turning he fled away no less quickly than he had appeared. But this brave monk followed hard on his heels as he escaped, and compelled him to seek refuge in his grave. This seemed promptly to open to him of its own accord, and when it had sheltered its inmate from his pursuer, it quickly closed over him.…

When they [the three other monks] heard the whole story, they at once decided that at the first break of day they must disinter this accursed corpse.… When they had cleared away the earth and brought the corpse to light they found it marked by a terrible wound, whilst the black blood that had flowed from this seemed to swamp the whole tomb. The carrion, therefore, was carried to a remote place outside the bounds of the monastery, where it was burned in a huge fire and the ashes scattered to the winds.

William of Newburgh
Historia Rerum Anglicarum
(A History of England), 1196
(quoted in Montague Summers
The Vampire in Europe, 1929)

In his work Relation d'un Voyage du Levant *(Account of a Journey to the Levant), published in 1717, French botanist Joseph Pitton de Tournefort (1656–1708) narrates the story of a* vrykolakas *believed to be haunting the Greek island of Mykonos.*

A Mischievous *Vrykolakas*

The one of whom I shall give an account was a peasant of Mykonos, naturally sullen and quarrelsome— a circumstance to be noted concerning such matters. He had been killed in the fields, no one knew by whom nor how. Two days after he had been buried in a chapel in the town, it was bruited about that he had been seen walking during the night, taking long strides; that he came into houses and turned over furniture, extinguished lamps, embraced people from behind, and played a thousand little roguish tricks.

An Island in Delirium

At first people only laughed, but the matter became serious when the most respectable people began to complain. Even the popes acknowledged the fact, and doubtless they had their reasons.

People did not fail to have masses said, but the peasant continued his little escapades without mending his ways. After a number of meetings of the town leaders and of the priests and monks, they concluded that it would be necessary—in accord with I don't know what ancient ceremony—to wait till nine days after the burial.

On the tenth day they said a mass in the chapel where the body lay, in order to drive out the demon that they believed to be concealed in it. The body was disinterred after the mass, and they set about the task of tearing out its heart. The butcher of the town, quite old and very maladroit, began by opening the belly rather than the chest. He rummaged about for a long time in the entrails, without finding what he sought, and finally someone informed him that it was necessary to cut into the diaphragm. The heart was torn out to the admiration of all the bystanders. But the body stank so terribly that incense had to be burned, but the smoke, mixed with the exhalations of this carrion, did nothing but increase the stench, and it began to inflame the minds of these poor people.

Their imagination, struck by the spectacle, filled with visions. They took it into their heads to say that a thick smoke was coming from the body, and we did not dare say that it was the incense. People kept calling out nothing but "Vrykolakas!" in the chapel and in the square before it, this being the name they give to these supposed revenants. The noise spread through the streets as if it were being roared, and this name seemed to be invented to shake the vault of the chapel. Several of the bystanders claimed that the blood of this unfortunate man was quite red,

Detail of *Hell,* a painting by Hans Memling, a 15th-century Flemish painter.

ourselves near the cadaver to make our observations as precisely as possible, we almost perished from the great stench that emerged from it. When they asked us what we thought of the deceased, we answered that we thought him quite adequately dead. But because we wanted to cure—or at the least not to irritate their stricken imaginations—we represented to them that it was not surprising if the butcher had perceived some warmth in rummaging about in the entrails, which were putrefying; that it was not extraordinary if fumes were emitted, just as such emerge from a dung heap when one stirs it up; and as for the pretended red blood, it was still evident on the hands of the butcher that this was nothing but a stinking mess.

After all our reasoning, they were of a mind to go to the seashore and burn the heart of the deceased, who, in spite of this execution became less docile and made more noise than ever. They accused him of beating people at night, of breaking in doors, and even roofs; of breaking windows, tearing up clothes, and emptying pitchers and bottles. He was a very thirsty dead man: I believe that he did not spare any house but that of the consul, with whom we lodged.

An End to the Evil Spell

So then they carried the vrykolakas, by the order of the administrators, to the tip of Saint George's Island, where a great funeral pyre had been prepared, with tar, out of fear that the wood, as dry as it was, would not burn fast enough for them on its own. The remains of this unfortunate cadaver were thrown on and consumed in a short time (this was the first of January, 1701). We saw the fire as we returned from Delos. You could call it a true fire of rejoicing, for

and the butcher swore that the body was still warm, from which they concluded that the deceased had the severe defect of not being quite dead, or, to state it better, of letting himself be reanimated by the devil, for that is exactly the idea they have of a vrykolakas. They caused this name to resound in an astonishing manner. And then there arrived a crowd of people who professed loudly that they had plainly seen that the corpse had not become stiff when they carried it from the fields to the church to bury it, and that as a result it was a true vrykolakas. That was the refrain.

I do not doubt that they would have maintained that the body did not stink, if we had not been present, so stunned were these poor people from the business, and so persuaded of the return of the dead. As for us, who had placed one no longer heard the complaints against the vrykolakas. They were content to observe that the devil had certainly been caught this time, and they composed a few songs to ridicule him.

Tournefort's Conclusion

In the whole archipelago people are persuaded that it is only the Greeks of the Orthodox Church whose corpses are reanimated by the devil. The inhabitants of the island of Santorini are terribly afraid of such types of werewolves, and the people of Mykonos, after their visions had dissipated, were equally afraid of prosecution by the Turks and by the bishop of Tinos. Not a single pope wanted to be present at Saint George, when they burned the body, out of fear that the bishop would exact a sum of money for their having exhumed and burned the deceased without his permission.

As for the Turks, it is certain that, at their first visit, they did not fail to make the community of Mykonos pay for the blood of this poor devil, who became in every way an abomination and horror to his country. And after that, is it not necessary to point out that the Greeks of today are not the great Greeks, and that there is among them only ignorance and superstition!

Joseph Pitton de Tournefort
Relation d'un Voyage du Levant
vol. 1, 1717
(quoted in Paul Barber, *Vampires, Burial and Death,* 1988)

It was the Arnold (or, in Serbian, Arnod) Paole affair in Serbia, recorded in 1732 by physician Johann Flückinger in a document entitled Visum et Repertum *(Seen and Reported), that truly made the vampire known throughout western Europe.*

After it had been reported that in the village of Medvegia the so-called vampires had killed some people by sucking their blood, I was…sent there to investigate the matter thoroughly, along with officers detailed for that purpose and two subordinate medical officers, and therefore carried out and heard the present inquiry in the company of the captain of the Stallath Company of haiduks [a type of soldier], Gorschiz Hadnack, the bariactar [literally: standard-bearer] and the oldest haiduk of the village, as follows: who unanimously recount that about five years ago a local haiduk by the name of Arnod Paole broke his neck in a fall from a hay wagon.

This man had, during his lifetime, often revealed that…he had been troubled by a vampire, wherefore he had eaten from the earth of the vampire's grave and had smeared himself with the vampire's blood, in order to be free of the vexation he had suffered…. [A]fter his death some people complained that they were being bothered by this same Arnod Paole; and in fact four people were killed by him. In order to end this evil, they dug up this Arnod Paole forty days after his death…; and they found that he was quite complete and undecayed, and that fresh blood had flowed from his eyes, nose, mouth, and ears; that the shirt, the covering, and the coffin were completely bloody; that the old nails on his hands and feet, along with the skin, had fallen off, and that new ones had grown; and since they saw from this that he was a true vampire, they drove a stake through his heart, according to their custom, whereby he gave an audible groan and bled copiously. Thereupon they burned the body the same day to ashes and threw these into the grave. These same people say further that all those who were tormented and killed by the vampires must themselves become vampires. Therefore they disinterred the above-mentioned four people in the same way. Then they also add that this Arnod Paole attacked not only the people but also the cattle, and sucked out their blood.

Johann Flückinger
Visum et Repertum, 1732
(quoted in Paul Barber, op. cit.)

In his 1746 treatise (published in English in 1850 under the title The Phantom World: History and Philosophy of Spirits and Apparitions*), 17th-century French philosopher and theologian Dom Augustin Calmet cites this letter addressed to one of his friends on the subject of a vampire in Hungary.*

In order to satisfy the questions of his Reverence Father Calmet concerning vampires, the undersigned has the

honor of assuring him that there is nothing truer nor more certain than those of which he has undoubtedly read in the public records and documents that have been inserted in the gazettes throughout Europe; but of all the public records that have appeared, his Reverence should take as absolutely truthful and plain that of the deputation of Belgrade appointed by SMI [his imperial majesty] the late Charles VI, of glorious memory, and executed by His Serene Highness the late Duke Charles Alexander of Württemberg, at the time viceroy or governor of the kingdom of Serbia; but I cannot for the present give the year, nor the month, nor the day, for want of my papers, which are nowhere near me at the moment.

This prince caused a deputation to depart from Belgrade, composed of half military officers, half civilian officials, with the General Auditor of the kingdom, to travel to a village where an infamous vampire deceased for many years had been wreaking excessive havoc among his kind, for note that it is only within their family and among their own relations that the bloodsuckers delight in destroying our species. This deputation counted among its members men and subjects celebrated for their good character and even by their learning, irreproachable and even scholarly, among the two orders: they were sworn and accompanied by a lieutenant of the grenadiers from the regiment of Prince Alexander of Württemberg and twenty-four grenadiers of his regiment.

Every honest man, including the duke himself, that could be found in Belgrade joined this deputation to act as eyewitnesses to the truth of the proof I am about to unfold.

Once arrived on the scene, they found that in the space of fifteen days, the vampire, uncle to five nephews and nieces, had already dispatched three, as well as one of his own brothers. He was working on the fifth, a beautiful young woman, his niece, and had already sucked her [blood] twice before an end

A 1539 wood engraving depicting the Greek goddess Persephone being kidnapped by Hades, god of the underworld.

was put to this sad tragedy by the following operations.

They removed themselves with the delegated commissioners not far from Belgrade, in a village, in public view, at nightfall, to his tomb. This gentleman could not tell me the circumstances surrounding the bloodsucking of the earlier dead, nor any particulars on the subject. This person, after having his blood sucked, found himself in a pitiful state of languor, weakness, lassitude, the agony was so violent. It was about three years ago that he was buried; on his tomb shone a light resembling that of a lamp, but less strong. The tomb was opened and inside was found a man, still whole and seemingly as healthy as any among us, the eyewitnesses; the hair on his head and his body, his fingernails, teeth, and eyes (these half-closed) as securely attached to him as they were to us, who have life and existence, and his heart was beating.

Then the corpse was pulled from the tomb, his body in truth not very supple, but lacking no part, neither flesh nor bones; then his heart was pierced with a sort of round and pointed iron spear: out of it came some whitish liquid matter along with the blood, but there was more blood than matter, none of it having any kind of bad odor; then his head was cut off with an ax similar to that used in England for executions: out of it came also the same kind of matter and blood that I just described, but more abundantly in proportion to that which flowed from the heart. In addition, quicklime was forcefully thrown on the grave to consume [the remains] more quickly; and from that time his niece, whose blood had been sucked twice, got better.

An illustration for *Varney the Vampyre,* 1847.

At the site where these people had been sucked a strong bluish spot forms; the exact location of the bloodsucking was not determined, as it is as much in one place as another. This is a notorious fact affirmed by the most authentic records, and which happened in sight of more than 1300 persons most deserving of credit.

But I intend, in order to satisfy more fully the curiosity of the learned Father Calmet, to describe in detail what I have seen on this subject with my own eyes, and send it to his sire the knight of Saint-Urbain to turn over to him, as delighted in this as in all other things to find opportunities to prove to him that there exists no one with a more perfect veneration and respect than his very humble and obedient servant L. de Beloz, formerly captain in the regiment of HSH the late Prince Alexander of Württemberg, and his aide-de-camp, and presently first captain of grenadiers in the regiment of the baron of Trenck.

Dom Augustin Calmet,
*Traité sur les Apparitions des Esprits et
sur les Vampires,*
1746

French Romantic novelist and playwright Prosper Mérimée (1803–70) purported to have witnessed this incident of vampirism while on a trip to Serbia.

Testimony of Prosper Mérimée

One night, the two women of the house having left us about an hour ago and to avoid drinking, I was singing for my host several songs of his country, when we were interrupted by horrible shrieks coming from the bedroom; normally, there is only one in the house, and it serves everyone.

We ran there armed and came upon a frightful spectacle. The mother, pale and disheveled, supported her even paler daughter, who had fainted and was stretched out on a bale of hay that served as a bed. She cried, "A vampire! A vampire! My poor child is dead!"

Our united efforts managed to bring back her poor Khava. She had seen, she told us, the window open and a man, pale and swathed in a shroud, threw himself on her and bit her in his attempt to strangle her. At the screams she managed to produce, the specter fled and she fainted.

Meanwhile, she had recognized as the vampire a man of the country, dead over fifteen days and named Wieczany. She had on her neck a small red mark; but I cannot say if this was a natural mark or if some insect had not bitten her during her nightmare.…

At dawn the entire village was stirring. The men were armed with guns and hatchets. The women carried red-hot irons. The children had stones and sticks. They took themselves to the cemetery in the midst of cries and injuries that they heaped on the deceased. I had a job of it to force my way through this enraged crowd and find a place near the grave.… Just as the sheet covering the body was lifted, a horribly piercing shriek made my hair stand on end: it was uttered by a woman beside me: "It's a vampire! He's not eaten by the worms!" and one hundred mouths repeated this at once.

At the same time twenty gunshots fired simultaneously blew the head of the corpse to pieces, and the father and family of Khava struck it repeatedly with their long knives. The women mopped up with sheets the red liquid that oozed from the mangled body with the aim of rubbing it on the neck of the stricken.

Meanwhile, several young men dragged the body out of the grave, and even though it was riddled with blows they took the precaution of tying it securely to the trunk of a pine tree; then they trailed it, followed by all the children, to a small orchard across from the house. There, prepared earlier, were sticks and straw intermingled. They set the fire, then threw the cadaver into it and began to dance around and competed in cries.…

The neck of the invalid was wrapped with the rags stained with the red and stinking liquid that they took for blood and which made a horrible contrast with the half-nude throat and shoulders of the poor Khava.

Prosper Mérimée
La Guzla
1827
(quoted in Tony Faivre, op. cit.)

The Rationalist Response

The scientists, philosophers, and theologians of the 18th century—embracing the new rationalist spirit of the Enlightenment—strongly condemned the stories of vampires that were appearing in all sorts of publications and pseudoscientific treatises.

Renowned French satirist Voltaire (1694–1778) gave free rein to his indignation and fierce humor regarding the belief in bloodsucking revenants in an article entitled "Vampires" that he included in his 1764 Dictionnaire Philosophique. *(An English edition,* Philosophical Dictionary, *was published in 1852.)*

Belief in Vampires Is an Anachronism

What! is it in our eighteenth century that vampires exist? Is it after the reigns of [philosopher John] Locke, [Locke's pupil Anthony Ashley Cooper, 3rd earl of] Shaftesbury, Trenchard, and [theologian Anthony] Collins? Is it under those of [Jean Le Rond] d'Alembert, [Denis] Diderot, [Jean François de] St. Lambert, and [Charles-Pinot] Duclos, that we believe in vampires, and that the reverend father Dom [Augustin] Calmet, benedictine

An 18th-century engraving of festivities on Walpurgisnacht, a German witches' sabbath traditionally held on May Day eve.

priest of the congregation of St. Vannes and St. Hidulphe, abbé of Senon,—an abbey of a hundred thousand livres a year, in the neighborhood of two other abbeys of the same revenue,—has printed and reprinted the history of vampires, with the approbation of the Sorbonne, signed Marcilli?

These vampires were corpses, who went out of their graves at night to suck the blood of the living, either at their throats or stomachs, after which they returned to their cemeteries. The persons so sucked waned, grew pale, and fell into consumptions; while the sucking corpse grew fat, got rosy, and enjoyed an excellent appetite. It was in Poland, Hungary, Silesia, Moravia, Austria, and Lorraine, that the dead made this good cheer.

We never heard speak of vampires in London, nor even at Paris. I confess that in both these cities there were stock-jobbers, brokers, and men of business, who sucked the blood of the people in broad day-light; but they were not dead, though corrupted. These true suckers lived not in cemeteries, but in very agreeable palaces.

Monks Are the Only True Vampires

The kings of Persia were, said they, the first who caused themselves to be served with viands after their death. Almost all the kings of the present day imitate them, but they are the monks who eat their dinner and supper, and drink their wine. Thus, properly speaking, kings are not vampires: the true vampires are the monks, who eat at the expense of both kings and people.

It is very true, that St. Stanislaus, who had bought a considerable estate from a Polish gentleman, and not paid him for it, being brought before king

Boleslas, by his heirs, raised up the gentleman; but this was solely to get quittance. It is not said that he gave a single glass of wine to the seller, who returned to the other world without having eaten or drunk. They afterwards treated of the grand question, whether a vampire could be absolved who died excommunicated, which comes more to the point. I am not profound enough in theology to give my opinion on this subject, but I would willingly be for absolution, because in all doubtful affairs we should take the mildest part.

There Are Now No More!

The result of all this is, that a great part of Europe has been infested with vampires for five or six years, and that there are now no more; that we have had convulsionaries in France for twenty years, that we have them no longer; that we have had demoniacs for seventeen hundred years, but have them no longer; that the dead have been raised ever since the days of Hippolytus, but that they are raised no longer; and lastly, that we have had jesuits in Spain, Portugal, France, and the two Sicilies, but that we have them no longer.

Voltaire
Philosophical Dictionary, 1852

In 1755, the chief physician to Empress Maria Theresa of Austria, Gérard Van Swieten, sent his employer a medical report condemning belief in vampires.

An English Vampire

Some months ago I read a small English treatise printed in London, in 1751, in which one could read of a notable and well-proven fact. In the month of February 1750, the tomb of an old family in the county of Devonshire in

Maria Theresa, empress of Austria.

England was opened: among many bones and numerous rotting caskets was found an intact wooden box: it was opened out of curiosity; within was found the whole body of a man: the flesh yet retained its natural firmness; the joints of the shoulders, neck, and fingers were completely supple: when the face was pressed, it gave under the finger but regained its shape as soon as the pressure lifted: the same thing was tried on the entire body; the beard was black, and four inches long. The cadaver had not been embalmed, as no sign of incision was spotted. There you have an English vampire, which for 80 years had rested peacefully in its tomb, bothering no one.

Superstition, Daughter of Ignorance

Let us examine the alleged facts offered as proof of vampirism. Rosina Iolackin,

died 22 December 1754, was dug up on 19 January 1755 and declared a vampire fit for the fire, because she was found intact in her tomb. In the winter, anatomists keep cadavers in the open air for six weeks and even two months without putrefaction. And it is worth noting that this winter has been particularly harsh.

Most of the bodies of all the other unearthed cadavers had already decomposed: but it sufficed that they were not completely putrefied, so, quick, into the fire! What ignorance!... Two sterilization specialists, "surgeons" who had never seen a dried-up cadaver, who knew nothing of the structure of the human body, as they themselves confessed to the commissioners, were

A scene at a funeral ceremony in England in the 18th century.

the witnesses who were to establish the sentence of fire....

It is on bases of this sort that this entire story has been concocted, that sacrileges are being committed, and that the sanctuary of tombs is being violated; discredit has been heaped on the reputation of the dead and their families, who have only the same sort of treatment to look forward to, if such abuses do not gradually disappear: to the hands of the executioners are thrown the bodies of children expired in innocence; men whose manner of life gave not the least suspicion of having the misfortune to be dug up, simply because a supposed witch had been placed in the earth.

They are declared witches; not only are their bodies given over to the executioner, so that they will be reduced to ashes, but their sentence emphasizes that they will have been much more severely punished than if they were still alive; and that their bodies be burned with infamy, to set an example for their accomplices.

Where are the laws that authorize such judgments? It is admitted that they do not exist, but it is coldly asserted that custom demands them. What a shower of disasters! Such things upset me and put me in such a fury that I must here end my account before I overstep the bounds of decency.

Gérard Van Swieten
(quoted in Roger Vadim
Histoires de Vampires, 1963)

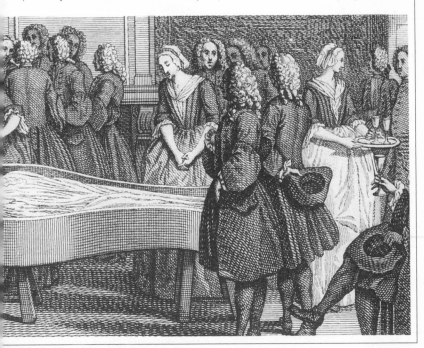

The Vampire in Poetry

Well before its introduction into prose literature, the vampire—or more precisely, the femme fatale in the guise of a vampire—had intrigued and inspired poets all over Europe.

German poet Johann Wolfgang von Goethe wrote Die Braut von Corinth *(The Bride of Corinth) in 1797. In the denouement, the young revenant reveals her true identity to her lover of a night.*

In his sudden fright, the youthful lover
Tries the flimsy veil the maid has shed,
Tries the carpet for his love as cover,
She unwinds, at once, what he has
    spread.
As with ghostly might,
To her fullest height,
Slowly she lifts up her form in bed.

"Mother," says she—hollow sounds her
    chiding—
"Thou dost grudge a night beside my
    groom!
Thou dost drive me from this cosy
    biding,
Have I wakened only to my doom?
Not enough thou vowed
Me into the shroud,
And so soon hast brought me to the
    tomb?

…

"He, this youth, was pledged to me by
    token,
When still Venus' temples graced the
    land.
But thy word, O mother, thou hast
    broken,
At a false, and foreign vow's command!
Yet no god forbears
When a mother swears,
To refuse her daughter's promised hand.

"From the silent graveyard I am driven,
Still to seek the joys I missed,—though
    dust—,

A*n Elegant Lady*, a painting by Briès.

Still to love him, who from me was riven.
Suck his life-blood from his heart with
  gust.
Once he is destroyed,
Others are decoyed,
And the young fall victims to my lust.

"Handsome youth, to death thou hast
  awoken!
Thou wilt pine away here, in despond.
I have given thee my chain as token,
And I take thy lock of hair as bond.
Look at it today,
Morrow finds thee gray,
Brown-haired thou appear'st in the
  beyond.

"Mother, this my last wish, is
  compelling:
Build a pyre! Let this be thy aim!
Open up my small and narrow dwelling,
Lay the lovers to their rest in flame!
While the sparks still fly,
Ere the embers die,
We, above, the ancient gods acclaim."
            Johann Wolfgang von Goethe
            Die Braut von Corinth
translated by Helen Kurz Roberts, 1980

*In 1857, just as Charles-Pierre Baudelaire's
collection of poems* Les Fleurs du Mal
*(The Flowers of Evil) was about to be
published, six of the poems were deemed by
the censors to be immoral and obscene and
had to be suppressed. "Les Métamorphoses
du Vampire" (Metamorphoses of the
Vampire) was one of these. (It was
reinstated in later editions.)*

The woman, meanwhile, writhing like
  a snake
across hot coals and hiking up her
  breasts
over her corset-stays, began to speak

as if her mouth had steeped each word
  in musk:
"My lips are smooth, and with them I
  know how
to smother conscience somewhere in
  these sheets.
I make the old men laugh like little boys,
and on my triumphant bosom all tears
  dry.
Look at me naked, and I will replace
sun and moon and every star in the sky.
So apt am I, dear scholar, in my lore
that once I fold a man in these fatal
  arms
or forfeit to his teeth my breasts which
  are
timid and teasing, tender and tyrannous,
upon these cushions swooning with
  delight
the impotent angels would be damned
  for me!"

When she had sucked the marrow from
  my bones,
and I leaned toward her listlessly
to return her loving kisses, all I saw
was a kind of slimy wineskin brimming
  with pus!
I closed my eyes in a spasm of cold fear,
and when I opened them to the light of
  day,
beside me, instead of that potent
  mannequin
who seemed to have drunk so deeply of
  my blood,
there trembled the wreckage of a
  skeleton
which grated with the cry of a
  weathervane
or a rusty signboard hanging from a
  pole,
battered by the wind on winter nights.
            Charles-Pierre Baudelaire
      "Les Métamorphoses du Vampire"
translated by Richard Howard, 1982

The Vampire in Prose

Dracula, *which inspired so many novels, stories, and films, is the text on which the modern myth of the vampire is based. This character is not exclusively male, however, as attested by two other masterpieces of 19th-century literature—French writer and critic Théophile Gautier's 1857 "La Morte Amoureuse" (translated as* The Vampire in 1901) *and the short story "Carmilla," written in 1872 by Irish novelist Joseph Sheridan Le Fanu.*

DRACULA

Our hero, Jonathan Harker, is sent on a mission to Count Dracula's castle in Transylvania. He describes in his journal the strange behavior of his host.

Harker Is Received by Dracula

The old man motioned me in with his right hand with a courtly gesture, saying in excellent English, but with a strange intonation:—

"Welcome to my house! Enter freely and of your own will!" He made no motion of stepping to meet me, but stood like a statue, as though his gesture of welcome had fixed him into stone. The instant, however, that I had stepped over the threshold, he moved impulsively forward, and holding out his hand grasped mine with a strength that made me wince, an effect which was not lessened by the fact that it seemed as cold as ice—more like the hand of a dead than a living man. Again he said:—

"Welcome to my house. Come freely. Go safely; and leave something of the happiness you bring!"…

I said interrogatively:—

"Count Dracula?" He bowed in a courtly way as he replied:—

"I am Dracula; and I bid you welcome, Mr. Harker, to my house. Come in; the night air is chill, and you must need to eat and rest."

Portrait of Dracula

His face was a strong—a very strong—aquiline, with high bridge of the thin nose and peculiarly arched nostrils; with lofty domed forehead, and hair

Bram Stoker.

The meeting of Jonathan Harker (Peter Cushing) and Count Dracula (Christopher Lee), a still from the British film *Dracula* (1958), directed by Terence Fisher.

growing scantily round the temples, but profusely elsewhere. His eyebrows were very massive, almost meeting over the nose, and with bushy hair that seemed to curl in its own profusion. The mouth, so far as I could see it under the heavy moustache, was fixed and rather cruel-looking, with peculiarly sharp white teeth; these protruded over the lips, whose remarkable ruddiness showed astonishing vitality in a man of his years. For the rest, his ears were pale and at the tops extremely pointed; the chin was broad and strong, and the cheeks firm though thin. The general effect was one of extraordinary pallor.

Hitherto I had noticed the backs of his hands as they lay on his knees in the firelight, and they had seemed rather white and fine; but seeing them now close to me, I could not but notice that they were rather coarse—broad, with squat fingers. Strange to say, there were hairs in the centre of the palm. The nails were long and fine, and cut to a sharp point. As the Count leaned over me and his hands touched me, I could not repress a shudder. It may have been that his breath was rank, but a horrible feeling of nausea came over me, which, do what I could, I could not conceal. The Count, evidently noticing it, drew back; and with a grim sort of smile, which showed more than he had yet done his protuberant teeth, sat himself down again on his own side of the fireplace. We were both silent for a while; and as I looked towards the window I saw the first dim streak of the coming dawn. There seemed a strange stillness over everything; but as I listened I heard as if from down below in the valley the howling of many wolves. The Count's eyes gleamed, and he said:—

"Listen to them—the children of the night. What music they make!"

Dracula Reveals His Vampire Nature

I only slept a few hours when I went to bed, and feeling that I could not sleep any more, got up. I had hung my shaving glass by the window, and was just beginning to shave. Suddenly I felt a hand on my shoulder, and heard the Count's voice saying to me, "Good-morning." I started, for it amazed me that I had not seen him, since the reflection of the glass covered the whole room behind me. In starting I had cut myself slightly, but did not notice it at the moment. Having answered the Count's salutation, I turned to the glass again to see how I had been mistaken. This time there could be no error, for the man was close to me, and I could see him over my shoulder. But there was no reflection of him in the mirror! The whole room behind me was displayed; but there was no sign of a man in it, except myself. This was startling, and, coming on the top of so many strange things, was beginning to increase that vague feeling of uneasiness which I always had when the Count is near; but at the instant I saw that the cut had bled a little, and the blood was trickling over my chin. I laid down the razor, turning as I did so half round to look for some sticking plaster. When the Count saw my face, his eyes blazed with a sort of demoniac fury, and he suddenly made a grab at my throat. I drew away, and his hand touched the string of beads which held the crucifix. It made an instant change in him, for the fury passed so quickly that I could

hardly believe that it was ever there.

"Take care," he said, "take care how you cut yourself. It is more dangerous than you think in this country."

Dracula Crawls Along the Wall

What I saw was the Count's head coming out from the window. I did not see the face, but I knew the man by the neck and the movement of his back and arms. In any case I could not mistake the hands which I had had so many opportunities of studying. I was at first interested and somewhat amused, for it is wonderful how small a matter will interest and amuse a man when he is a prisoner. But my very feelings changed to repulsion and terror when I saw the whole man slowly emerge from the window and begin to crawl down the castle wall over that dreadful abyss, *face down*, with his cloak spreading out around him like great wings. At first I could not believe my eyes. I thought it was some trick of the moonlight, some weird effect of shadow; but I kept looking, and it could be no delusion. I saw the fingers and toes grasp the corners of the stones, worn clear of the mortar by the stress of years, and by thus using every projection and inequality move downwards with considerable speed, just as a lizard moves along a wall.

What manner of man is this, or what manner of creature is it in the semblance of man? I feel the dread of this horrible place overpowering me; I am in fear—in awful fear—and there is no escape for me; I am encompassed about with terrors that I dare not think of....

The Vampire in His Coffin

The great box was in the same place, close against the wall, but the lid was laid on it, not fastened down, but with

A vampire attacking its sleeping victim.

the nails ready in their places to be hammered home. I knew I must search the body for the key, so I raised the lid, and laid it back against the wall; and then I saw something which filled my very soul with horror. There lay the Count, but looking as if his youth had been half renewed, for the white hair and moustache were changed to dark iron-grey; the cheeks were fuller, and the white skin seemed ruby-red underneath; the mouth was redder than ever, for on the lips were gouts of fresh blood, which trickled from the corners of the mouth and ran over the chin and neck. Even the deep, burning eyes seemed set amongst swollen flesh, for the lids and pouches underneath were bloated. It seemed as if the whole awful creature were simply gorged with blood; he lay like a filthy leech, exhausted with his repletion.

Dracula, now in England, initiates Mina Harker into vampirism against her will. Here she describes to her husband and Professor Van Helsing the horrible scene.

The Baptism of Blood

"With a mocking smile, he placed one hand upon my shoulder and, holding me tight, bared my throat with the other, saying as he did so: 'First, a little refreshment to reward my exertions. You may as well be quiet; it is not the first time, or the second, that your veins have appeased my thirst!' I was bewildered, and, strangely enough, I did not want to hinder him. I suppose it is a part of the horrible curse that such is, when his touch is on his victim. And oh, my God, my God, pity me! He placed his reeking lips upon my throat!" Her husband groaned again. She clasped his hand harder, and looked at him pityingly, as if he were the injured one, and went on:—

"I felt my strength fading away, and I was in a half swoon. How long this horrible thing lasted I know not; but it seemed that a long time must have passed before he took his foul, awful, sneering mouth away. I saw it drip with the fresh blood!" The remembrance seemed for a while to overpower her, and she drooped and would have sunk down but for her husband's sustaining arm. With a great effort she recovered herself and went on:—

"Then he spoke to me mockingly, 'And so you, like the others, would play your brains against mine. You would help these men to hunt me and frustrate me in my designs! You know now, and they know in part already, and will know in full before long, what it is to cross my path. They should have kept their energies for use closer to home. Whilst they played wits against me—against me who commanded nations, and intrigued for them, and fought for them, hundreds of years before they were born—I was countermining them.

'And you, their best beloved one, are now to me, flesh of my flesh; blood of my blood; kin of my kin; my bountiful wine-press for a while; and shall be later on my companion and my helper. You shall be avenged in turn; for not one of them but shall minister to your needs. But as yet you are to be punished for what you have done. You have aided in thwarting me; now you shall come to my call. When my brain says "Come!" to you, you shall cross land or sea to do my bidding; and to that end this!' With that he pulled open his shirt, and with his long sharp nails opened a vein in his breast. When the blood began to spurt out, he took my hands in one of his, holding them tight, and with the other seized my neck and pressed my mouth to the wound, so that I must either suffocate or swallow some of the— Oh my God! my God! what have I done? What have I done to deserve such a fate, I who have tried to walk in meekness and righteousness all my days. God pity me! Look down on a poor soul in worse than mortal peril; and in mercy pity those to whom she is dear!" Then she began to rub her lips as though to cleanse them from pollution.

Bram Stoker
Dracula, 1897

"LA MORTE AMOUREUSE"

The young priest Romualdo, narrator of Gautier's short story, has been called to the bedside of the courtesan Clarimonda to administer the last rites, but he arrives too late: The young woman is dead.

Clarimonda on Her Deathbed

Shall I confess it? The perfection of her form, though refined and sanctified by the shadow of death, troubled me more voluptuously than was right, and her repose was so like sleep that any one might have been deceived by it. I forgot that I had come there to perform the funeral offices, and I imagined that I was a young husband entering the room of his bride who hides her face through modesty and will not allow herself to be seen. Sunk in grief, mad with joy, shivering with fear and pleasure, I bent towards her and took up the corner of the shroud; I raised it slowly, holding in my breath for fear of waking her. My arteries palpitated with such force that I felt the blood surging in my temples and my brow was covered with sweat as if I had been lifting a marble slab. It was indeed Clarimonda, such as I had seen her in the church on the day of my ordination. She was as lovely as then, and death seemed to be but a new coquetry of hers. The pallor of her cheeks, the paler rose of her lips, the long closed eyelashes showing their brown fringes against the whiteness, gave her an inexpressibly seductive expression of melancholy chastity and of pensive suffering. Her long hair, undone, in which were still a few little blue flowers, formed a pillow for her head and protected with its curls the nudity of her shoulders. Her lovely

A lover crying on the tomb of his beloved.

hands, purer and more diaphanous than the Host, were crossed in an attitude of pious repose and of silent prayer that softened the too great seduction, even in death, of the exquisite roundness and the ivory polish of her bare arms from which the pearl bracelets had not been removed.

Having become a vampire, Clarimonda seduces Romualdo. In order to deliver his young friend from her evil spell, Father Serapion brings him to the cemetery.

The End of Clarimonda

At last Serapion's pick struck the coffin, which gave out the dull, sonorous sound which nothingness gives out when it is touched. He pulled off the cover, and I saw Clarimonda, pale as marble, her hands clasped, her white shroud forming but one line from her head to her feet. A little red drop shone like a rose at the corner of her discoloured lips. Serapion at the sight of it became furious.

"Ah! there you are, you demon, you shameless courtesan! You who drink blood and gold!" and he cast on the body and the coffin quantities of holy water, tracing with the sprinkler a cross upon the coffin. The holy dew no sooner touched poor Clarimonda than her lovely body fell into dust and became only a hideous mass of ashed and half-calcined bones. "There is your mistress, my lord Romualdo," said the inexorable priest, as he pointed to the remains. "Are you now still tempted to go to the Lido and Fusino with your beauty?"

I bowed my head. Something had been shattered within me. I returned to my presbytery, and lord Romualdo, the lover of Clarimonda, left the poor priest with whom he had so long kept such strange company. Only the next night I saw Clarimonda. She said to me, as the first time under the porch of the church, "Unfortunate man! unfortunate man! What have you done? Why did you listen to that foolish priest? Were you not happy? What have I done to you, that you should go and violate my poor tomb and lay bare the wretchedness of my nothingness? All communion between our souls and bodies is henceforth broken. Farewell; you will regret me."

She vanished in air like a vapour, and I never saw her again.

Théophile Gautier
The Vampire
translated by F. C. Sumichrast, 1901

"CARMILLA"

Laura, daughter of an old English soldier who has retired in Styria, in central Austria, is drawn to the mysterious Carmilla, whom her father has taken in. She is at once fascinated and embarrassed by the troubling sensuality of her new friend.

Sibylline Observations

There was a coldness, it seemed to me, beyond her years, in her smiling melancholy persistent refusal to afford me the least ray of light….

It was all summed up in three very vague disclosures:

First.—Her name was Carmilla.

Second.—Her family was very ancient and noble.

Third.—Her home lay in the direction of the west.

She would not tell me the name of her family, nor their armorial bearings, nor the name of their estate, nor even that of the country they lived in….

But I must add this, that her evasion was conducted with so pretty a melancholy and deprecation, with so many, and even passionate declarations of her liking for me, and trust in my honour, and with so many promises that I should at last know all, that I could not find it in my heart long to be offended with her.

She used to place her pretty arms about my neck, draw me to her, and laying her cheek to mine, murmur with her lips near my ear, "Dearest, your little heart is wounded; think me not cruel because I obey the irresistible law of my strength and weakness; if your dear heart is wounded, my wild heart bleeds with yours. In the rapture of my enormous humiliation I live in your warm life, and you shall die—die, sweetly die—into mine. I cannot help it; as I draw near to you, you, in your turn, will draw near to others, and learn the rapture of that cruelty, which yet is love; so, for a while, seek to know no more of me and mine, but trust me with all your loving spirit."

And when she had spoken such a rhapsody, she would press me more closely in her trembling embrace, and her lips in soft kisses gently glow upon my cheek.

Laura's Agonies and Nightmares

Certain vague and strange sensations visited me in my sleep. The prevailing one was of that pleasant, peculiar cold thrill which we feel in bathing, when we move against the current of a river. This was soon accompanied by dreams that seemed interminable, and were so vague that I could never recollect their scenery and persons, or any one connected portion of their action. But they left an awful impression, and a sense of exhaustion, as if I had passed through a long period of great mental exertion and danger. After all these dreams there remained on waking a remembrance of having been in a place very nearly dark, and of having spoken to people whom I could not see; and especially of one clear voice, of a

female's, very deep, that spoke as if at a distance, slowly, and producing always the same sensation of indescribable solemnity and fear. Sometimes there came a sensation as if a hand was drawn softly along my cheek and neck. Sometimes it was as if warm lips kissed me, and longer and more lovingly as they reached my throat, but there the caress fixed itself. My heart beat faster, my breathing rose and fell rapidly and full drawn; a sobbing, that rose into a sense of strangulation, supervened, and turned into a dreadful convulsion, in which my senses left me, and I became unconscious.

It was now three weeks since the commencement of this unaccountable state. My sufferings had, during the last week, told upon my appearance. I had grown pale, my eyes were dilated and darkened underneath, and the languor which I had long felt began to display itself in my countenance.

My father asked me often whether I

was ill; but, with an obstinacy which now seems to me unaccountable, I persisted in assuring him that I was quite well.

In a sense this was true. I had no pain, I could complain of no bodily derangement. My complaint seemed to be one of the imagination, or the nerves, and, horrible as my sufferings were, I kept them, with a morbid reserve, very nearly to myself.

It could not be that terrible complaint which the peasants call the oupire, for I had now been suffering for three weeks, and they were seldom ill for much more than three days, when death put an end to their miseries.

Carmilla complained of dreams and feverish sensations, but by no means of so alarming a kind as mine. I say that mine were extremely alarming. Had I been capable of comprehending my condition, I would have invoked aid and advice on my knees. The narcotic of an unsuspected influence was acting upon me, and my perceptions were benumbed....

One night, instead of the voice I was accustomed to hear in the dark, I heard one, sweet and tender, and at the same time terrible, which said, "Your mother warns you to beware of the assassin." At the same time a light unexpectedly sprang up, and I saw Carmilla, standing, near the foot of my bed, in her white nightdress, bathed from her chin to her feet, in one great stain of blood.

Joseph Sheridan Le Fanu
"Carmilla"
Best Ghost Stories of J. S. Le Fanu
1964

Vampire bats attacking sleepers, in an illustration for *Wanderings in South America* (1826), by Charles Waterton.

INTERVIEW WITH THE VAMPIRE

In 1976, popular American novelist Anne Rice began to write a set of fictional "chronicles" that would soon bring her unexpected worldwide renown. And who is the charmingly diabolical protagonist of these chronicles that span the centuries? None other than a vampire, the French expatriate Lestat. Picking up where Bram Stoker left off, Anne Rice gives the timeless myth a 20th-century twist.

Recollections of a Demon

In an interview that takes place in San Francisco in the 1970s, a vampire named Louis describes to a very frightened young man how he was transformed into a vampire by Lestat in Louisiana in the year 1791. Here Louis recounts his second visitation from Lestat.

"It was very late, after my sister had fallen asleep. I can remember it as if it were yesterday. He came in from the courtyard, opening the French doors without a sound, a tall fair-skinned man with a mass of blond hair and a graceful, almost feline quality to his movements. And gently, he draped a shawl over my sister's eyes and lowered the wick of the lamp. She dozed there beside the basin and the cloth with which she'd bathed my forehead, and she never once stirred under that shawl until morning. But by that time I was greatly changed."

"What *was* the change?" asked the boy.

The vampire sighed. He leaned back against the chair and looked at the walls. "At first I thought he was another doctor, or someone summoned by the family to try to reason with me. But this suspicion was removed at once. He stepped close to my bed and leaned down so that his face was in the lamplight, and I saw that he was no ordinary man at all. His gray eyes burned with an incandescence, and the long white hands which hung by his sides were not those of a human being. I think I knew everything in that instant, and all that he told me was only aftermath. What I mean is, the moment I saw him, saw his extraordinary aura and knew him to be no creature I'd ever known, I was reduced to nothing. That ego which could not accept the presence of an extraordinary human being in its midst was crushed. All my conceptions, even my guilt and wish to die, seemed utterly unimportant. I completely forgot *myself!*" he said, now silently touching his breast with his fist. "I forgot myself totally. And in the same instant knew totally the meaning of possibility. From then on I experienced only increasing wonder. As he talked to me and told me of what I might become, of what his life had been and stood to be, my past shrank to embers. I saw my life as if I stood apart from it, the vanity, the self-serving, the constant fleeing from one petty annoyance after another, the lip service to God and the Virgin and a host of saints whose names filled my prayer books, none of whom made the slightest difference in a narrow, materialistic, and selfish existence. I saw my real gods…the gods of most men. Food, drink, and security in conformity. Cinders."

The boy's face was tense with a mixture of confusion and amazement. "And so you decided to become a vampire?" he asked. The vampire was silent for a moment.

"Decided. It doesn't seem the right

B ela Lugosi and Dwight Frye in the film
Dracula, 1931.

going to drain you now to the very threshold of death, and I want you to be quiet, so quiet that you can almost hear the flow of blood through your veins, so quiet that you can hear the flow of that same blood through mine. It is your consciousness, your will, which must keep you alive.' I wanted to struggle, but he pressed so hard with his fingers that he held my entire prone body in check; and as soon as I stopped my abortive attempt at rebellion, he sank his teeth into my neck."

The boy's eyes grew huge. He had drawn farther and farther back in his chair as the vampire spoke, and now his face was tense, his eyes narrow, as if he were preparing to weather a blow.

"Have you ever lost a great amount of blood?" asked the vampire. "Do you know the feeling?"

The boy's lips shaped the word *no,* but no sound came out. He cleared his throat. "No," he said....

"'Listen, keep your eyes wide,' Lestat whispered to me, his lips moving against my neck. I remember that the movement of his lips raised the hair all over my body, sent a shock of sensation through my body that was not unlike the pleasure of passion....'"

He mused, his right fingers slightly curled beneath his chin, the first finger appearing to lightly stroke it. "The result was that within minutes I was weak to paralysis. Panic-stricken, I discovered I could not even will myself to speak. Lestat still held me, of course, and his arm was like the weight of an iron bar. I felt his teeth withdraw with such a keenness that the two puncture wounds seemed enormous, lined with pain. And now he bent over my helpless head and, taking his right hand off me, bit his own wrist. The blood flowed

word. Yet I cannot say it was inevitable from the moment that he stepped into the room. No, indeed, it was not inevitable. Yet I can't say I decided. Let me say that when he'd finished speaking, no other decision was possible for me, and I pursued my course without a backward glance...."

Succumbing to Lestat's fiendish charm, Louis assists him with a murder and then asks to be killed himself.

"He put his right arm around me and pulled me close to his chest. Never had I been this close to him before, and in the dim light I could see the magnificent radiance of his eye and the unnatural mask of his skin. As I tried to move, he pressed his right fingers against my lips and said, 'Be still. I am down upon my shirt and coat, and he watched it with a narrow, gleaming eye.… He pressed his bleeding wrist to my mouth, said firmly, a little impatiently, 'Louis, drink.' And I did. 'Steady, Louis,' and 'Hurry,' he whispered to me a number of times. I drank, sucking the blood out of the holes, experiencing for the first time since infancy the special pleasure of sucking nourishment, the body focused with the mind upon one vital source. Then something happened." The vampire sat back, a slight frown on his face.

"How pathetic it is to describe these things which can't truly be described," he said, his voice low almost to a whisper. The boy sat as if frozen.…

"And then this next thing, this next thing was…sound. A dull roar at first and then a pounding like the pounding of a drum, growing louder and louder, as if some enormous creature were coming up on one slowly through a dark and alien forest, pounding as he came, a huge drum. And then there came the pounding of another drum.… And then Lestat pulled his wrist free suddenly, and I opened my eyes and checked myself in a moment of reaching for his wrist, grabbing it, forcing it back to my mouth at all costs; I checked myself because I realized that the drum was my heart, and the second drum had been his." The vampire sighed. "Do you understand?"

The boy began to speak, and then he shook his head. "No…I mean, I do," he said. "I mean, I…"

"Of course," said the vampire, looking away.

"Wait, wait!" said the boy in a welter of excitement. "The tape is almost gone. I have to turn it over." The vampire watched patiently as he changed it.

"What happened then?" the boy asked. His face was moist, and he wiped it hurriedly with his handkerchief.

"I saw as a vampire," said the vampire, his voice now slightly detached.

The vampire assures the boy that many of the characteristics traditionally ascribed to vampires are entirely false…

"Yes?" said the vampire. "I'm afraid I don't allow you to ask enough questions."

"I was going to ask, rosaries have crosses on them, don't they?"

"Oh, the rumor about crosses!" the vampire laughed. "You refer to our being afraid of crosses?"

"Unable to look on them, I thought," said the boy.

"Nonsense, my friend, sheer nonsense. I can look on anything I like. And I rather like looking on crucifixes in particular."

"And what about the rumor about keyholes? That you can…become steam and go through them."

"I wish I could," laughed the vampire. "How positively delightful. I should like to pass through all manner of different keyholes and feel the tickle of their peculiar shapes. No." He shook his head. "That is, how would you say today…bullshit?"

The boy laughed despite himself. Then his face grew serious.

"You mustn't be so shy with me," the vampire said. "What is it?"

"The story about stakes through

the heart," said the boy, his cheeks coloring slightly.

"The same," said the vampire. "Bull-shit," he said, carefully articulating both syllables, so that the boy smiled. "No magical power whatsoever...."

...while others are absolutely true.

"What happened then?" the boy asked. The vampire appeared to be watching the smoke gather beneath the overhead bulb.

"Ah...we went back to New Orleans posthaste," he said. "Lestat had his coffin in a miserable room near the ramparts."

"And you did get into the coffin?"

"I had no choice. I begged Lestat to let me stay in the closet, but he laughed, astonished. 'Don't you know what you are?' he asked. 'But is it magical? Must it have this shape?' I pleaded. Only to hear him laugh again. I couldn't bear the idea.... 'You're carrying on badly,' Lestat said finally. 'And it's almost dawn. I should let you die. You will die, you know. The sun will destroy the blood I've given you, in every tissue, every vein. But you shouldn't be feeling this fear at all. I think you're like a man who loses an arm or a leg and keeps insisting that he can feel pain where the arm or leg used to be.' Well, that was positively the most intelligent and useful thing Lestat ever said in my presence, and it brought me around at once. 'Now, I'm getting into the coffin,' he finally said to me in his most disdainful tone, 'and you will get in on top of me if you know what's good for you.' And I did. I lay face-down on him, utterly confused by my absence of dread and filled with distaste for being so close to him, handsome

and intriguing though he was. And he shut the lid. Then I asked him if I was completely dead. My body was tingling and itching all over. 'No, you're not then,' he said. 'When you are, you'll only hear and see it changing and feel nothing. You should be dead by tonight. Go to sleep.'"

Anne Rice
Interview with the Vampire
1976

Appearing only marginally human, Max Schreck played the lead in the 1922 German silent film *Nosferatu*, directed by F. W. Murnau.

A Night in Count Dracula's Castle

In 1977, American arcanologist and adventurer Vincent Hillyer was finally given permission by the Romanian government to fulfill one of his lifelong dreams—to spend a night in the ruins of Vlad Dracul Tepes' castle in Romania.

The birthplace of Vlad Dracul Tepes.

Hillyer's Arrival

At long last, there it was! The dying sun cast a blood-red glow upon the drifting fingers of fog that clutched at the brooding castle high atop the shadowy Carpathian ridge. Like some mysterious sentinel reaching into the darkening sky, the pale stone walls and decaying battlements stared menacingly down over the purple valley below. Castle Dracula, alone in its malefic majesty, grew more ominous by the minute!

[My guide] and my driver bade me good-bye.... [I] started climbing the 1531 roughly-hewn steps leading to the summit of this heavily forested mountain.... As I paused to catch my breath, I saw a narrow, rather frail looking drawbridge ahead, swinging a dizzying 1500 feet above the Arges River. It led to the great arched door of the castle. Frankly, in the gloom and wind, that little bridge didn't look very safe. But I had no choice. In spite of the growing cold I was deeply excited as I carefully crossed the chasm. I'd finally reached the stronghold of history's most famous vampire. Tonight I would be Dracula's guest! Then, for the first time, came a frightening thought. *Would I really meet my host?*

Inside the Castle

I lit my lantern, set my blanket roll down in the main hallway, and began unpacking my provisions.... My attention was suddenly diverted by the tumultuous flapping of wings high above in the black recesses of the ruined roof. *Bats!* Dozens of them!...

After watching and waiting for an

hour…my eyelids began to droop.… I lay down at the foot of the stairway and soon fell into a troubled sleep.…

I awoke abruptly, sensing something was wrong. Memory of [a] weird dream hung on, perplexing me. I lay thinking about its strange content, unconsciously reaching into the open neck of my shirt to rub at a mild pain on my collarbone. When I felt wetness, and looked at my fingertips, I was unnerved to see small drops of blood! But before I could sort out this odd turn of events I was shaken by the rush of alarm—a premonition. The sensation of being watched!… I rolled over and glanced down the moon-lit hallway. Through a large broken opening at the end I could see brightly twinkling stars.… Then it hit me. They weren't stars at all. *They were eyes! Watching me!*…

Curiosity soon overcame my concern. I rose, turned the wick higher on my lantern, and proceeded cautiously down the cavernous passageway. [The eyes were] casually observing my approach. … I swallowed hard. At any moment I expected to hear a low, foreign voice boom out: "VELCOME!"

What I found upon reaching the wall totally surprised me. A large, gray-muzzled wolf had thrust its head through the opening, looking as astonished as I was. The beast quickly bolted back down the mountainside into the protective cloak of night. It wasn't the castle's *master* after all.…

Then came the odd odor. It spread through the long chamber, reeking of decaying flowers. Strange, because there were *no* flowers growing on this barren, rocky peak. Further sleep was out of the question. The wind blew harder. I was chilled to the bone. It was only an hour until sunrise. I knew I'd have to leave before I froze to death.…The Romanian authorities had warned me that on no account was I to traverse the woods until daylight. But I had to make a choice.… I decided to go.

The Descent from the Mountain

Though the sun was indeed rising, its faintly dawning rays did not penetrate the thick foliage of the black forest. Darkness and gloom still engulfed my route deep inside the treacherous woods. Fortunately there was still sufficient fuel to keep my lantern lit.…

On my arrival at the inn, I went directly to the dining room. My guide was already breakfasting with several local officials. When I entered, they looked up, surprise and alarm on their faces.…That's when the natural adrenaline that had sustained me up until then abruptly gave out. My arms hung limply at my sides. My stomach wrenched. Droplets of cold sweat stung my eyes. I really felt rotten, and thought I was going to collapse.The Romanians jumped up as my guide called for the driver. "Get the car ready! We're taking Mr. Hillyer to the hospital!" And so, off we sped to the Curtea de Arges Clinic.

The puncture wounds the doctor discovered? Well, he *said* they must be the nasty bites of one of the giant spiders that infest the castle—one that apparently had shared my blanket.… The scent of decaying flowers? Later I learned that such a circumstance usually indicated an evil presence.…

Those "puncture wounds" still baffle me.… Those noticeable bites, *if correctly diagnosed,* could only have been made by an *exceptionally* large spider.…

Dracula's little joke?

Vincent Hillyer
Vampires, 1988

The Vampire in Film

The theme of the vampire has inspired hundreds of films all over the world. Uneven in quality, most of them are presented as cinematic adaptations of well-known literary texts— but this usually functions only as a nominal pretext.

The First Vampire Stars

The supernatural creature of evil came into its own with *Nosferatu, A Symphony of Horror* (1922), a German adaptation of Bram Stoker's *Dracula*. Even today, with any number of Draculas to look back on, Max Schreck as Orlock, the Dracula figure, is memorably nasty. The makeup, the walk, the eyes all have nothing to do with humanity. And there are other elements in the film those used to the conventions of the many later Dracula movies would find surprising, such as the self-sacrificing death of the heroine, who keeps Orlock by her side until sunrise, and the vampire-inspired plague that devastates Bremen.

It was, however, the 1931 *Dracula* starring Bela Lugosi—the first major talking film of supernatural horror— that set the pattern for decades to come. For the first time of many we heard the touchstone line, "Listen to them—the children of the night. What music they make!" delivered in the rich Middle European accents of the Count, referring to the howling of the wolves outside his Transylvanian castle.

Lugosi's performance and the legend of Dracula made a stunning impact. Despite endless variations on the theme, some of them brilliant in their own right, Dracula will always be the urbane Lugosi.

A Surrealist Vampire Tale

Carl Dreyer's *Vampyr* (1932) must be mentioned, but it presents the inevitable problems of the real artist…who bases his work on a theme usually confined to popular entertainment. *Vampyr* is a classic to the cinéaste, but it is highly likely to send the moviegoer in search of a good horror film into a state of either torpor of confusion, due to

Klaus Kinski and Isabelle Adjani in Werner Herzog's *Nosferatu the Vampyre* (1979).

the many touches of surrealism Dreyer used throughout the film.... But for those who value aesthetics above simple narrative thrills, *Vampyr* is an extraordinary experience, so far as can be judged from the poorly dubbed and badly edited prints available.

Dracula's Offspring

Dracula's Daughter [1936] is atypical in that it continues directly from the climax of its predecessor [and] is almost on the level of the original. The script, decor, and camerawork all show signs of sophistication. Gloria Holden has enormous presence as Marya, with a world-weary, seductive languor quite appropriate to the daughter of Lugosi's Count. Her wardrobe ranges from the expected cowled cloaks to *haute couture* deco gowns in which she looks the stunning embodiment of the exotic adventuress.

Vampire Humor

A hapless nineteenth-century apprentice encountering a mad variety of vampires, including a Jewish one on whom the cross doesn't work and a homosexual one on which his charms do (not that he wants them to), might seem more of a light fantasy than a dark one, and indeed Roman Polanski's *The Fearless Vampire Killers* (1967) had a lot of laughs. However, it didn't gain them at the expense of the genre conventions, and it was as spooky as it was spoofy. Polanski, who also starred as the young man forever gurgling in panic as both his blood and virtue are constantly threatened, showed brilliant comedic gifts, and Jack MacGowran as the dithering vampire-hunting professor was nearly as funny.

Modern Draculas

A new *Dracula* (1979) stuck much closer to the Stoker novel than the Lugosi version and gave us the silken Frank Langella of the beautiful voice as the vampire.... And David Bowie and the ageless Catherine Deneuve were a striking pair of modern vampires in *The Hunger* (1983), beautifully photographed if not totally believable.

Baird Searles
Films of Science Fiction and Fantasy, 1988

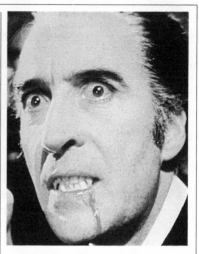

A gallery of canines. From left to right: Max Schreck (1922), Christopher Lee (1958), David Peel (1960), and Klaus Kinski (1979).

Filmography

1922 *Nosferatu: A Symphony of Horror* (German title: *Nosferatu: Eine Symphonie des Grauens,* directed by F. W. Murnau (Germany). With Max Schreck, Alexander Granach, Gustav von Wangenheim, and Greta Schroeder

1931 *Dracula,* directed by Tod Browning (United States). With Bela Lugosi, Helen Chandler, Dwight Frye, and Edward Van Sloan

1935 *Mark of the Vampire,* directed by Tod Browning (United States). With Bela Lugosi, Carol Borland, and Lionel Barrymore

1936 *Dracula's Daughter,* directed by Lambert Hillyer (United States). With Gloria Holden and Edward Van Sloan

1958 *Dracula* (American title: *Horror of Dracula*), directed by Terence Fisher (Great Britain). With Christopher Lee, Peter Cushing, and Carol Marsh

1960 *Brides of Dracula,* directed by Terence Fisher (Great Britain). With David Peel, Peter Cushing, Martita Hunt, and Yvonne Monlaur

1960 *Et Mourir de Plaisir* (American title: *Blood and Roses*), directed by Roger Vadim (France). With Annette Vadim, Elsa Martinelli, and Mel Ferrer

1960 *La Maschera del Demonio* (The Demon's Mask), directed by Mario Bava (Italy). With Barbara Steele, John Richardson, and Ivo Garrani

1965 *Dracula, Prince of Darkness,* directed by Terence Fisher (Great Britain). With Christopher Lee, Andrew Keir, and Barbara Shelley

1967 *The Fearless Vampire Killers, or Pardon Me, But Your Teeth Are in My Neck,* directed by Roman Polanski (Great Britain/United States). With Roman Polanski, Sharon Tate, Ferdy Mayne, and Jack McGowran

1970 *Countess Dracula,* directed by Peter Sasdy (Great Britain). With Ingrid Pitt, Nigel Green, Lesley-Anne Down, and Sandor Eles

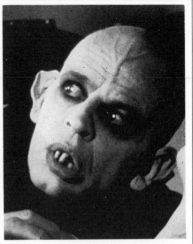

1970 *House of Dark Shadows,* directed by Dan Curtis (United States). With Jonathan Fridd, Grayson Hall, and Kathryn Leigh Scott

1971 *Count Dracula,* directed by Jesus Franco (Germany/Italy/Spain). With Christopher Lee, Herbert Lom, and Klaus Kinski

1971 *Les Lèvres Rouges* (The Red Lips), directed by Harry Kummel (Belgium/Germany/France). With Delphine Seyrig, Daniele Quinet, and Fons Rademakers

1974 *Andy Warhol's Dracula,* directed by Paul Morrissey (Italy). With Udo Kier, Vittorio de Sica, and Arno Juerging

1976 *Dracula, Père et Fils* (Dracula, Father and Son), directed by Eduard Molinero (France). With Christopher Lee, Bernard Menez, and Marie-Helene Breillat

1979 *Dracula,* directed by John Badham (United States). With Frank Langella, Laurence Olivier, Kate Nelligan, and Donald Pleasence

1979 *Love at First Bite,* directed by Stan Dragoti (United States). With George Hamilton, Susan St. James, and Richard Benjamin

1979 *Nosferatu the Vampyre* (German title: *Nosferatu, Phantom der Nacht*), directed by Werner Herzog (Germany/France). With Klaus Kinski, Isabelle Adjani, and Bruno Ganz

1983 *The Hunger,* directed by Tony Scott (United States). With Catherine Deneuve, David Bowie, and Susan Sarandon

1987 *The Lost Boys,* directed by Joel Schumacher (United States). With Jason Patric, Corey Haim, Dianne Wiest, and Kiefer Sutherland

1987 *Near Dark,* directed by Kathryn Bigelow (United States). With Jenny Wright, Leance Heriksen, and Adrian Pasdan

1992 *Bram Stoker's Dracula,* directed by Francis Ford Coppola (United States). With Gary Oldman, Winona Ryder, Anthony Hopkins, and Keanu Reeves

Bela Lugosi, in two films by Tod Browning: *Dracula* (1931), with Helen Chandler (above); and *Mark of the Vampire* (1935), with Carol Borland (opposite below).

Women, victims, or accomplices? The vampire's three mistresses in Tod Browning's *Dracula*.

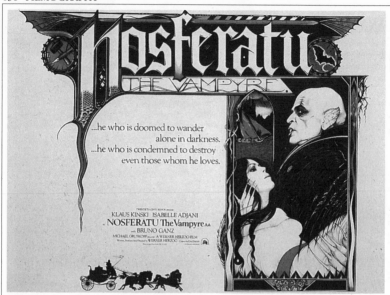

A poster for the American version of Werner Herzog's 1979 film *Nosferatu the Vampyre* (above). Ferdy Mayne and Sharon Tate in Roman Polanski's 1967 film *The Fearless Vampire Killers* (below).

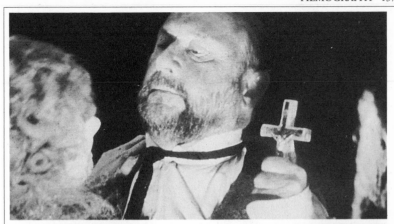

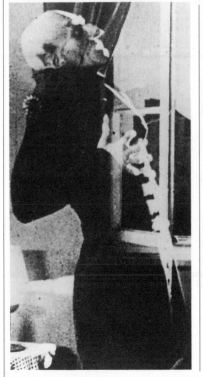

Clockwise from above: Kate Nelligan and Donald Pleasence in John Badham's *Dracula* (1979); Frank Langella in the same movie; Max Schreck in F. W. Murnau's *Nosferatu* (1922).

Further Reading

Auerbach, Nina, *Woman and the Demon: The Life of a Victorian Myth*, Cambridge University Press, Cambridge, England, 1982

Barber, Paul, *Vampires, Burial and Death: Folklore and Reality*, Yale University Press, New Haven, Connecticut, 1988

Berenbaum, Linda B., *The Gothic Imagination: Expansion in Gothic Literature and Art*, Fairleigh Dickinson University Press, Cranbury, New Jersey, 1982

Bleiler, E. F., ed., *Three Gothic Novels*, Dover, New York, 1966

Bojarski, Richard, *The Complete Films of Bela Lugosi*, Citadel Press, Secaucus, New Jersey, 1992

Briggs, Julia, *Night Visitors: The Rise and Fall of the English Ghost Story*, Faber & Faber, London, 1977

Calmet, Dom Augustin, *Traité sur les Apparitions des Esprits et sur les Vampires ou les Revenants de Hongrie, de Moravie, etc.*, 2 vols., Paris, 1751 (English edition: *The Phantom World: History and Philosophy of Spirits and Apparitions*, A. Hart, Philadelphia, 1850)

Carter, Margaret L., *Shadow of a Shade: Vampirism in Literature*, Gordon Press, New York, 1974

Copper, Basil, *The Vampire: In Legend and Fact*, Citadel Press, Secaucus, New Jersey, 1989

Dunn Mascetti, Manuela, *Vampire: The Complete Guide to the World of the Undead*, Viking Studio Books, New York, 1992

Faivre, Tony, *Les Vampires*, Losfeld, Paris, 1962

Farson, Daniel, *The Man Who Wrote Dracula: A Biography of Bram Stoker*, St. Martin's Press, New York, 1975

Florescu, Radu, and Raymond T. McNally, *Dracula, Prince of Many Faces: His Life and His Times*, Little, Brown, New York, 1990

———, *In Search of Dracula*, Warner Books, New York, 1973

Frayling, Christopher, *Vampyres: Lord Byron to Count Dracula*, Faber & Faber, London, 1992

Gautier, Théophile, "La Morte Amoureuse" (1857), translated as "The Vampire" in *The Works of Théophile Gautier*, vol. 11, George D. Sproul, New York, 1901

Gould, Charles, *Mythical Monsters*, Outlet Book Company, Avenal, New Jersey, 1989

Haining, Peter, *The Dracula Scrapbook*, New English Library, London, 1976

Hillyer, Vincent, *Vampires*, Loose Change Publications, Los Banos, California, 1988

Le Fanu, Joseph Sheridan, *Best Ghost Stories of J. S. Le Fanu*, Dover, New York, 1964

Masters, Anthony, *Natural History of the Vampire*, G. P. Putnam's Sons, New York, 1972

Murphy, Michael J., *The Celluloid Vampires: A History and Filmography, 1897–1979*, Pierian Press, Ann Arbor, Michigan, 1979

Riccardo, Martin, *Vampires Unearthed: The Vampire and Dracula Bibliography of Books, Articles, Movies, Records and Other Material*, Garland Publishers, New York, 1983

Rice, Anne, *The Vampire Chronicles*, 4 vols., Ballantine, New York, 1989

Ronay, Gabriel, *The Truth About Dracula*, Madison Books, Lanham, Maryland, 1974

Ryan, Alan, *The Penguin Book of Vampire Stories*, Viking Penguin, New York, 1987

Searles, Baird, *Films of Science Fiction and Fantasy*, Abrams, New York, 1988

Senf, Carol A., *The Vampire in Nineteenth-Century English Literature*, Bowling Green State University Popular Press, Ohio, 1988

Senn, Harry A., *Were-Wolf and Vampire in Romania*, East European Monographs, Boulder, Colorado, 1982

Stoker, Bram, *Dracula* (1897), in *The Essential Dracula*, ed. Leonard Wolf, Plume, New York, 1993

Summers, Montague, *The Vampire in Europe*, University Books, Inc., New Hyde Park, New York, 1968

Twitchell, James B., *The Living Dead: A Study of the Vampire in Romantic Literature*, Duke University Press, Durham, North Carolina, 1981

Vadim, Roger, *Histoires de Vampires*, Laffont, Paris, 1963

Villeneuve, Roland, *Loups-Garous et Vampires*, Bordas, Paris, 1991

Voltaire, *Philosophical Dictionary*, J. P. Mendum, Boston, 1852

Wright, Dudley, *The Book of Vampires*, Omnigraphics, Inc., Detroit, 1989

List of Illustrations

Key: a=above; b=below; c=center; l=left; r=right

Abbreviations:
BAD=Bibliothèque des Arts Décoratifs, Paris; BN=Bibliothèque Nationale, Paris

Front cover Henry Fuseli. *The Nightmare.* Painting, 1782. Frankfurt Museum
Spine Ian Kolonics. Count Dracula (detail). Illustration from the Hungarian periodical *Boszorkany* (Budapest), 1990
Back cover French poster for the British film *Dracula*, directed by Terence Fisher, 1958
1l Detail of a still from the American film *The Hunger*, directed by Tony Scott, 1983
1r Illustration in Bram Stoker, *Dracula*, 1897
2 Simon Marsden. Photograph, 1988
2–3 Detail of an illustration in Stoker's *Dracula*
3 Silhouette made from a still from the German film *Nosferatu*, directed by F. W. Murnau, 1922
4 *Idem*
4–5 Detail of an illustration in Stoker's *Dracula*
5 Simon Marsden. Photograph, 1988
6 *Idem*
6–7 Detail of an illustration in Stoker's *Dracula*
8–9 *Idem*
9a Silhouette made from a still from the German film *Nosferatu*, directed by F. W. Murnau, 1922

9b Simon Marsden. Photograph, 1988
11 Bats. Wood engraving from Alfred Brehm, *Die Säugetiere* (The Mammals), 1893
12 Sacrifice to a god. Indian miniature, 18th century. BN
13 Wooden figure of the kind placed in front of houses to keep away evil spirits. Nicobar Islands, Indian Ocean. Horniman Museum, London
14 Henri Regnault. *Summary Execution under the Moorish Kings of Granada.* Painting, 1870. Musée d'Orsay, Paris
15a Human sacrifice among the Aztecs. Miniature in a manuscript by Diego Durán, 1579
15b The sorceress Medea rejuvenating her lover, Jason. Engraving, 16th century. BAD
16 Lamia carrying a victim. Bas-relief, Greece, c. 400 BC. British Museum, London
16–7 Zeus turning Lycaon into a wolf. Engraving, 17th century. BN
17 Siren. Detail of a painting on a Greek *stamnos* (water jar), c. 490 BC. British Museum, London
18–9 Laurent de la Hyre. Abraham preparing to sacrifice his son Isaac. Painting, 17th century. Musée des Beaux-Arts, Reims, France
19 Persian amulet used to protect newborns from the bloodsucking demon Lilith. Wolfson Museum, Hechal Shlomo, Jerusalem

20 Christ on the cross. Ex-voto painting on wood, 19th century. Bayerisches Nationalmuseum, Munich
21a Paolo Uccello. *The Profanation of the Host.* Painting, 1467–9. Galleria Nazionale delle Marche, Urbino, Italy
21b *The Crucifixion.* Painting on wood, 15th or 16th century. Bayerisches National-museum, Munich
22 *The Resurrection of the Dead.* Miniature from a set of gospels by Vysehrard, c. 1085. National Library and University, Prague
22–3 Luca Signorelli. *The Last Judgment* (detail). Painting, 1499–1502. Dome of the Chapel of the Madonna of San Brizio, Orvieto, Italy
23a *The Last Judgment: The Devils* (detail). Romanian icon from Transylvania, 1832. Muzeul National de Arta al României, Bucharest
23b A. Sorg. A young man from the island of Rhodes discovering a demon in the tomb of his fiancée. Wood engraving, 1481. Augsberg, Germany
24 *Demons Spreading an Epidemic.* Miniature. BN
24–5a Pietro Lorenzetti. *Tyranny.* Fresco, 13th century
24–5b Gilles de Muisit. *The Plague at Tournai.* Miniature, 1349. Bibliothèque Royale, Brussels
26 Gilles de Rais's seal
26–7 Houtnagel. *Hungarians Impaled by the Turks.* Colored engraving, 1617. BN

27 Vlad Tepes. Painting. Kunsthistorisches Museum, Vienna
28 Vlad Tepes. Wood engraving, c. 1550. Nuremberg, Germany
29 Vlad Tepes, "the Impaler." Wood engraving, 1500. Strasbourg, France
30 *The Triumph of Death.* Painting, 15th century, Flanders. Musée du Berry, Bourges, France
31 Guyot Marchant. *Danse Macabre.* Woodcut, 1486. Paris
32 Scenes of cruentation in *Diebold's Chronicle of Lucerne.* Middle Ages. Bibliothèque Centrale, Lucerne, Switzerland
33a Hans Baldung Grien. *The Knight, the Maiden, and Death.* Painting, early 16th century. Musée du Louvre, Paris
33b Witches roasting a child. Wood engraving, 1626
34 Erzsebet Báthory. Painting, 19th century. Andras Dabasi/Magyar Nemzeti Galéria (National Museum, History Gallery), Budapest
34–5 Itsvan Csok. *Erzsebet Báthory Putting Young Women to Death.* Painting, 19th century. Szépmüvészeti Múzeum (Museum of Fine Arts), Budapest
36–7 Castle Csejthe in upper Hungary, residence of Erzsebet Báthory. Postcard, early 20th century
38 Gaston le Vuilliers. *The Tatra Mountains.* Engraving in *Le Tour du Monde,* vol. 1, 1881

Index

Photograph Credits

Archiv für Kunst und Geschichte, Berlin 28, 57r, 106–7. Archives Jean Marigny 1r, 2–3, 4–5, 6–7, 8–9, 76–7, 78, 79, 83, 88. Bibliothèque Centrale, Lucerne 32. Bibliothèque Nationale, Paris 16–7, 24, 50–1a, 51b, 59, 60, 61a, 61b, 62, 63, 70, 70–1, 71b, 72–5, 76, 82al, 82ar, 94l. Bildarchiv Preussischer Kulturbesitz, Berlin 42–3b. Bridgeman, London 66, 66–7, 68, 86. British Film Institute, London 84–5, 86–7, 91a, 136a, 136b, 137bl. Jean-Loup Charmet, Paris 12, 15b, 16, 23a, 26–7, 36–7, 40a, 40b, 47b, 54l, 77, 81bl, 81br, 88–9, 96, 121, spine. Cinémathèque Française, Paris 131, 134. Ciné-plus, Paris back cover. Collection Christophe L., Paris 92, 117, 133r, 135a, 135b, 137a, 137br. Andras Dabasi, Budapest 34. Dagli Orti, Paris 15a, 17, 22, 24–5a, 26. Edimedia, Paris 24–5b, 53, 91b. Film Museum, Munich 90, 132l. Giraudon, Paris 22–3, 33a, 44, 46, 47a. Claus Hansmann, Munich 11, 20, 21b, 23b, 41a, 45, 56al. Harris Publications, Inc., New York 95a, 95b. Vincent Hillyer, California 128. Michael Holford, London 13. Jacana/Parès 86–7 background. Hubert Josse, Paris 14, 18–9, 64, front cover. Kunsthistorisches Museum, Vienna 27. Lauros Giraudon, Paris 21a, 30. Szepsy Szucs Levante, Budapest 100. Magnum/Erich Lessing, Paris 41b. Simon Marsden, London 2, 5, 6, 9b. Mary Evans Picture Library, London 29, 33b, 55, 82b, 98, 108, 110, 112, 116, 119, 122–3. Musées Royaux des Beaux-Arts de Belgique, Brussels 48–9. Muséum National d'Histoire Naturelle, Paris 54r. Museum of Fine Arts, Budapest 34–5. National Portrait Gallery, London 71a. Elise Palix, Paris 81a, 104, 132r, 133l. Roger Viollet, Paris 56br, 112–3, 114. Scala, Florence 80

Text Credits

Grateful acknowledgment is made for use of material from the following: Paul Barber, *Vampires, Burial, and Death: Folklore and Reality.* Yale University Press, 1988. Reproduced by permission of the publisher (pp. 103–6); Charles-Pierre Baudelaire, *Les Fleurs du Mal,* translated by Richard Howard. David R. Godine, Boston, Massachusetts, 1982. Reprinted by permission of David R. Godine Publishers, Inc. (p. 115); Johann Wolfgang von Goethe, *The Eternal Feminine: Selected Poems of Goethe,* edited by Frederick Ungar. Copyright © 1980 by The Frederick Ungar Publishing Company. Reprinted by permission of The Continuum Publishing Company, New York (pp. 114–5); Vincent Hillyer, *Vampires,* Loose Change Publications, Los Banos, California, 1988 (pp. 128–9); Joseph Sheridan Le Fanu, *Best Ghost Stories of J. S. Le Fanu,* edited by E. F. Bleiler. Dover, New York, 1964 (pp. 122–3); Anne Rice, *Interview with the Vampire.* Copyright © 1976 by Anne O'Brien Rice. Reprinted by permission of Alfred A. Knopf, Inc. (pp. 124–7); Baird Searles, *Films of Science Fiction and Fantasy,* Harry N. Abrams, Inc., New York, 1988 (pp. 130–1); Bram Stoker, *Dracula,* reprinted in *The Essential Dracula,* by Leonard Wolf, Plume, New York, 1993 (pp. 116–20); Montague Summers, *The Vampire in Europe,* University Books, New Hyde Park, New York, 1968. Reproduced by permission of the publisher. Published by arrangement with Carol Publishing Group, New York (pp. 101, 102–3)

Jean Marigny teaches English at Stendhal University in Grenoble, France, where he also directs a research center for studies in fantasy and horror in English and American literature. In addition to his doctoral dissertation, Marigny has published numerous articles and books on the subject of vampires.

To John William Polidori

Translated from the French by Lory Frankel

Project Manager: Sharon AvRutick
Typographic Designer: Elissa Ichiyasu
Editor: Jennifer Stockman
Design Assistant: Miko McGinty
Text Permissions: Neil Ryder Hoos

Library of Congress Catalog Card Number: 93–72811

ISBN 0–8109–2869–8

Copyright © 1993 Gallimard

English translation copyright © 1994 Harry N. Abrams, Inc., New York, and Thames and Hudson Ltd., London

Published in 1994 by Harry N. Abrams, Incorporated, New York
A Times Mirror Company

Printed and bound in Italy by Editoriale Libraria, Trieste